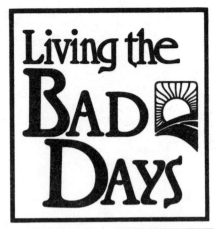

Living the BAD Days

Why They Come
and How to Survive

Living the BAD DAYS

Why They Come and How to Survive

James Allen Sparks

ABINGDON/NASHVILLE

LIVING THE BAD DAYS

Copyright © 1982 by Abingdon

Library of Congress Cataloging in Publication Data

SPARKS, JAMES ALLEN, 1933–
  Living the bad days.
  1. Depression, Mental.   I. Title.
  RC537.S63   158'.1   81-10951   AACR2

ISBN 0-687-22290-7

MANUFACTURED BY THE PARTHENON PRESS AT
NASHVILLE, TENNESSEE, UNITED STATES OF AMERICA

It is still raining outside, and the clock is ten minutes fast. The youngest child has dropped her bacon into her milk, and "I knew what kind of a day it was going to be," my wife says, "the minute I caught my sleeve on that damned knob."

—Frederick Buechner, *The Alphabet of Grace*

What do we possess save faith that there is a God, a time of hereafter; that there may be a way that all events, all things, have meaning?

—Robert E. Gard, *An Innocence of Prairie*

Contents

Personal Notes

Everyone has bad days. Down days. Blue days. Under-the-weather days. Unhappy days. Alone, miserable, out-of-sync days.

Having a bad day is like playing a pinball game that's just taken our last quarter, and then "tilts." The play's all over—at least for that day. When the "tilt" sign lights up, a good day has soured. No matter how much we yell, push, or hammer on it, the game is over. Like the steel ball that knocks against the lifeless bumpers of a tilted pinball game, we bump up against family, friends, and the people we work with. But the day is lifeless. The joy is gone.

On bad days, we look around to see who's free of such hassles. Surely everyone has bad days, we tell ourselves, but somehow, *ours* must be the worst. We search the eyes of the stranger on the street, look over the drugstore smorgasbord of tranquilizers, and daydream of finding the answer to our unhappiness and distress. But bad days come quickly, slipping in without warning. They depart slowly.

Example: It is a cold winter's night. The furnace breaks down. You call the repairman. He says he will "put you on the list," and might get to your furnace the next afternoon. You're furious. But at whom? The repairman who doesn't understand? Or at yourself? Maybe you have put off cleaning the furnace, and now feel guilty and unhappy about that. A whole list of "I-wish-I-hads" feeds guilt. Though the sun has not risen upon tomorrow, you feel a bad day coming.

Big crises cause bad days. We expect that. Somehow we find strength and faith to press on in the face of serious illness, death, or other major adversities.

But it's those unexpected tilts, the kind that sneak up on us, that do us in. It's the little irritations—the frustrations, resentments, threats, and loneliness—that drain us, dissipate our energies, and turn good days bad.

You may be reading this book because that's how you feel. Or you may have just survived a bad day. Or you may know a bad day is coming. Perhaps you hope this book will give some answers, or help you cope.

I have written this book to be a companion as you suffer through your bad days. I have drawn from many sources, people who let us see their pain as they've tried to cope with bad days. Also I offer my own personal perspective, because I trust it—the "back porch" wisdom I've learned in dealing with bad days.

If this is a gray and gloomy day for you, through these pages I come as a friend who invites you to draw close, who puts an arm around your shoulder, who gives you permission to hurt and maybe cry a little. *You are not alone!* I write not as a philosopher, an all-knowing parent, a psychologist, or a preacher, but as a fellow-sojourner along the way. I too have felt out-of-control and powerless in the bad days. Looking back on other bad days, I see that I struggled against them as if they were the enemy, not seeing that they might have value and meaning beyond their temporary pain.

I bring a point of view that encourages *acceptance* of bad days rather than *resistance*. I hope you will use such days actively, refocus your life, tune in on the messages spoken by your inner self, examine how you are *being* in the world, and tap your own inner strength.

There's something else, too. Despite all the suggestions for living through the bad days, some problems just keep on. Even a strong faith in God (if you are a religious person), a loving family, steadfast friends, and a sense that we've done what's right can't fix some situations, regardless of what we do. We feel frustrated and helpless. What then?

I have some suggestions along the lines of what the British have revered as the ultimate strategy for handling the impossible—"muddling through." It's what H. L. Mencken, journalist and cynic during the early 1900's, called "skill at dealing with the inevitable." Each chapter offers advice for coping with the more common bad days, and the final chapter is on muddling through when everything else fails.

In preparing this manuscript, I am grateful (looking back, of course) to all the bad days that have helped me appreciate the good. And to Sheila Mulcahy and Rita Sears who helped prepare the manuscript, keeping good days from turning sour.

Madison, Wisconsin
July, 1981

Introduction

Does Everyone Have Bad Days?

A recent visit with some psychiatrist friends proved what most of us know in our heads but haven't accepted deep down—that no one has it together all of the time.

Joanna and Mark, husband and wife, both psychiatrists, came to our house for dinner the other evening. Joanna looked tired when she took off her coat, having spent the morning at the hospital talking to a young woman bent on killing herself. During dinner, the question came up, "Do psychiatrists have bad days?"

"Doctors aren't supposed to have bad days," Joanna said. "People feel cheated if you admit to having one, especially if they have an appointment on that day."

Joanna—to my surprise—did not link her bad days with trying to keep people from killing themselves or treating people who think the Soviet secret police are after them. Her bad days, like many of ours, have to do with the irritating but not so serious problems, like an unexplained pain in the elbow, a teenaged son who stays out too late, or a fight with a relative.

That makes our friends Joanna and Mark ordinary people and fun to trade anxieties with—the anxieties that fiftyish types swap as often as brown liver spots mysteriously appear in the bathroom mirror. When we get together, we try to outdo each other as to who has the biggest crisis. No one has to lie on a couch or be interrupted at the end of the hour. They don't play doctor, and I don't preach.

While Joanna and Pauline were clearing the table, Mark leaned close, and with the concentration of a doctor answering an emergency, said, "Jim, you're a man of the cloth. . . ."

Something in the way he said it made me blurt out, "I think you're putting me on."

"No, I'm quite serious," he said. "I've got a personal problem that's really getting to me."

"This must be serious," I thought, feeling a little embarrassed at being so flippant, and hoping I wouldn't appear too shocked when he laid out the sordid details of some involved case.

"It's my car," he said. "It's only seven months old, and the dealer has given up on it. I've written letters—I've tried niceness and nastiness—but I can't get any satisfaction. I don't know where to turn."

My face must have betrayed my disappointment as I tried to down-shift an over-accelerated pulse. All set to solve a heady problem, to do battle with a demon that had out-psyched the medical profession, and to bring years of seasoned clergy experience to bear on an important case! I pulled back in wounded pride. "A broken engine! What kind of problem is that?" I thought.

I had missed the point! The fouled engine was only incidental to Mark's real concern—his frustration over a minor, annoying problem. He had tried all the good advice he gives people who confront difficult situations, and it had made no difference. Frustration had turned to anger. He had a new car with a patched-up engine. Powerless to do anything more, he felt himself a victim of the same mindless, impersonal detachment that creates a need for psychiatrists in the first place. "What do I do now?" the doctor asked.

Bad Days Point to a Real World Out There

Mark's professional role of psychiatrist helped him little with his wounded car. Irritation and frustration overrode more than ten years of training. Like all of us who come to the end of our knowledge or patience, Mark asked, "What do I do now?"

"The most 'real' world we live in is that of our fellow human beings," wrote *Small Is Beautiful* author, E. F. Schumacher. He said, "Without them we should experience a sense of enormous emptiness; we could hardly be human ourselves, for we are made or marred by our relations with other people." And because we are human, he said, we are all subject to human conditions like hesitating, doubting, changing our minds, running hither and yon, uncertain of how to get where we want to go, even uncertain of what we want.[1]

No wonder bad days get us down. When we combine all the mistakes other people make with those we make ourselves, the potential for bad days is limitless. We think something's wrong with *us*, and that somewhere "out there" are people who never have it quite as bad as we do. This daydream is like a piece of shrapnel broken off the old American happiness myth. It has misled generations with the promise that someday life will be trouble-free.

Another piece of the illusion is that certain people, because of who they are and what they do, have fewer problems than the rest of us. Psychiatrists, clergy, psychologists, and educators, according to this idea, have built-in exemptions. Maybe it has something to do with the idea that we believe happiness is related to how much a person knows, and that these occupations guarantee not only knowledge, but also wisdom.

Mark's dilemma, however, illustrates how the real world is—one problem-solving situation right after the other, for psychiatrists and everybody else. No one escapes.

Psychiatrists have bad days and feel temporarily off-center in their world, too. But we expect them to dispense happiness to themselves as well as to their patients—and that they will be living testimonials to their own therapy. There seems to be a driving hunger within the American spirit that demands the 100 percent solution, the perfect road map for getting through life. In our eternal pursuit of this illusion, we believe that "out there" is the perfect book, the perfect doctor, the perfect religion, the perfect guru, or the perfect formula that will open the door of life and carry us into a land where the sun always shines.

Yet it is the existence of problems created by the real world of fallible and imperfect people that affirms our existence—our "aliveness." To be free of problems is to be dead.

Many of our bad days are related to mixed-up and messed-up between-people things—disagreements between friends, misunderstandings between spouses, and conflicts with co-workers, for example.

When asked what he or she considers the reason for bad days, everyone names something different. One person said she has a bad day when she feels fragmented and pulled in different directions by too many conflicting demands. Another connects bad days to having certain expectations and finding that he cannot meet them. A young professor has a bad day when his carelessness makes him angry at himself for his "stupidity." No one I talked to pointed to the larger life-cycle crises. Most people I talked to thought a day was bad if it was filled with frustration, resentments, or some type of threat, whether emotional, occupational, financial, or physical.

My brother Frank, an Ohio minister, knows he's going to have a bad day when that all-too-familiar, needle-like twinge strikes his lower back. Another kidney stone is sure to be on its way down the urinary tract, the culprit in many emergency trips to the hospital and five major surgeries. Scars lace his stomach like tracks in a railroad switching yard.

He knows the routine: when symptoms appear, call the clinic, instruct his secretary about next Sunday's service, pack pajamas, and drive to the hospital. Of course, there's always an outside chance that the doctor will not see a white dot on the x-ray film, that the pain is nothing more than a pulled muscle, and he can go home. But the doctor's grim expression has too often meant, "Frank, that stone has to go."

My brother has been in this situation so many times that he has learned what to expect—from the bottoming out of his stomach at hearing the verdict, to how to survive catheters and other surgery unpleasantness. The last time he missed only one Sunday service. When I suggest that his operations must seem no more bothersome than an impacted wisdom tooth, his response is almost unprintable. Frank has consulted the big name kidney clinics in the country, but the mystery continues. Unable to find the cure, he lives with a continuing, nagging frustration. Now that he and the surgeons no longer fight it, he recovers more quickly.

Bad Days Connect Us to a Timeless Wisdom

Any time we struggle with a bad day, we join all who have gone before us who have also suffered. It's important to know that we're not alone in our distress. This knowledge may not ease us over the crisis, but it does help us understand and accept the price of being human. Let's look at two key ideas:

Bad days are inescapable. The human capacity for pain and suffering goes back to the Creation, and is a dominant theme of the Judeo-Christian scriptures. To love is to be open to hurt. To love is to live—to experience the world by being affected, changed, transformed, and turned around by people who love us back. A person's capacity for joy is only as great as his or her capacity for suffering.

"Human life is alive to the extent that it is loved and affirmed," says German theologian Jürgen Moltmann. "The more passionately we love life, the more intensively we experience the joy of life. The more passionately we love life, the more we also experience the pain of life and the deadliness of death. We experience joy and pain, we become alive and mortal at one and the same time. . . ."[2]

The Bible affirms the inevitability of our being open, accessible, and possibly hurt by the "real world," which we often experience as a bad day. The emphasis, however, is on living through the bad days—not giving in or giving up on them.

God has bad days too. If you find it difficult to believe that society's custodians of the happy life—psychiatrists and others—have bad days, imagine God having them. God not only created people to be happy, but gave them psychiatrists to help them find that happiness. Where God got into trouble was in getting mixed up with people in the first place. The whole Creation thing was going pretty well until he got to people. Here's how the Genesis author describes God's bad days: "Yahweh saw that the wickedness of man was great on the earth, and that the thoughts in his heart fashioned nothing but wickedness all day long. Yahweh regretted having made man on the earth, and his heart grieved" (6:7).

The late Jean-Paul Sartre, believing that individuals are responsible for themselves in spite of the tragically absurd human condition, has dramatically expressed his own despair of humankind in a one-act play. The characters have died and gone "below." What they find does not fit their Dantean images of Hell. In the last few moments of "No Exit," Garcin says to his companions: ". . . You remember all we were told about the torture chambers, the fire and brimstone, the 'burning marl.' Old wives' tales! There's no need for red-hot pokers. Hell is—other people!"[3]

Sartre's cynicism is overwhelming, but understandable. Most of us have known that "hell" is strained or broken relationships, unresolved conflicts, and months or years of backed-up anger and resentment. We also know the frustration of looking on as bystanders while some wrong or injustice rewards the perpetrator and harms an innocent victim.

Theologian Moltmann speculates about God's bad days:

> I once regarded as childish and human—all too human—
> the Old Testament ideas of a God who fumed with rage,
> who was jealous, who burned with love and could be
> disillusioned. The abstract god of the philosophers,
> purified of all human images, seemed to me nearer to the
> truth. But the more I experienced how abstraction
> destroyed life, the more I understood the Old Testament
> passion of God, and the pain which tore his heart. I was
> deeply moved to hear Jews say that the real suffering in the
> persecution of Israel was the suffering of God. God suffers
> with Israel. He goes with his people into exile, into

concentration camps, into the gas chamber, into death. Their faith in the God who suffered with them preserved Israel against desperate self-destruction and against self-surrender through accommodation. When we discover in the depths of our own suffering the suffering of God we cannot become apathetic. . . .[4]

We can only conclude that God has bad days because he also stands with *us* as we live through our bad days; that he suffers with the agnostic as well as with the devout believer; that his pain is the hurt of an involved participant.

Yet, in spite of such time-tempered assurances, our suffering often outweighs our ability to be rational and objective about it—or even to appreciate any potential or ultimate spiritual consolation. Regardless of what we may learn from religion or psychiatry, each bad day is ours to live through and make the most of.

Part One
What Bad Days Are Made Of

Author Allen Wheelis says what many of us have known all along: "It's better . . . to have one big problem than a bagful of small ones." Big problems we can see and feel. It's the little ones that scoot around and make life miserable. We never know where those little nuisances will pop up. They are like summer colds that hang on for weeks. We don't get sick enough to go to bed, but we want to. We try the usual home remedies—a night's sleep, a hot toddy, or an hour or two of TV-induced anesthesia. The ache subsides for a while, but then comes back.

Big problems versus a bagful of small ones are like big rocks compared to a heap of pebbles. They may be the same weight, but pebbles are more difficult to handle. A rock can be picked up and moved. Pebbles are more like melting gelatin that rolls around the spoon and falls off. Try to carry pebbles on a shovel across your lawn and most of them will roll off into the grass. They clog the lawnmower and become dangerous missiles when hit. They anger and frustrate us because they are so unpredictable. So are the "little" irritations and problems that bad days are made of.

In this section we look at what bad days are made of—frustrations, resentments, threats to our security, and loneliness. While these represent the more common causes of bad days, anything that puts us on "tilt" will qualify.

1

Frustration: When We Can't Get Our Way

"There are a few things in life you can always depend on," writes Andy Rooney, a syndicated columnist and television essayist for CBS.

> It is common knowledge, for example, that any line you choose to stand in for anything will be the slowest to move. At the bank, you get behind someone with a whole payroll to work out in pennies; at the supermarket, you choose the line in which people don't seem to have much in their carts, but it turns out that two of the six people ahead of you have to have checks validated. . . .[1]

He goes on to list eighteen other everyday frustrations that tease out our anger when we can't get what we want as quickly as we want it.

In this chapter we shall see how frustration, a cornerstone of bad-day feelings, can turn a good day topsy-turvy.

Feeling Frustrated

Frustration is wanting something and not getting it. It's having all systems ready for the rocket launching and then aborting the launch because a red warning light signals that a twenty-five-cent screw is missing on the nose cone. It's preparing for a long-awaited trip only to have the water pump on the car go out. It's sending in the mortgage payment and finding out it's been lost in the mail. It's saving up for a new washing machine, but having it break down the day after you buy it. It's having a problem and discovering there's no one who cares or is even willing to listen. Or, as the stress researcher, Hans Selye, has said, it's being dissatisfied with the way your life is going. As a person grows older and presses toward the climax of a career, he or she may doubt the importance of what his or her life has been and grumble about missed opportunities and look for someone to blame. Behind these complaints lies the frustrating sensation that there could have been more and the fault is really theirs.[2]

Once, when people lived closer to the earth, their frustration had to do with too much rain or too little, or with how soon a farmer could get the corn planted. It also had to do with the ordinary frictions and irritations that arose between people who lived and worked together, who depended upon each other for their survival. It's what makes novels and plays come to life and draws us to the next page or the third act. If our frustrations were limited only to these "normal" and expected potential aggravations, they might not bother us so much.

But it's the "not-so-normal" aggravations—the ones that hit us on our blind side when we're not looking—that make us feel out-of-control, unable to find a rational solution. It's as if life sometimes defies rationality, and then we discover that we have become victims rather than participants. The very technology that saves time and paperwork can also age us overnight through excessive worry and irritation. For example, that modern miracle— the computer—can be a blessing or a curse. If you make a mistake or are late with a payment, this mindless labyrinth of transistors and circuits will hound you to the end and stubbornly refuse to listen when you try to talk to it about a problem of its own creation. Recently, a Pentagon computer alerted U.S. military strike units that the Soviets had launched attack missiles twice in the same week. Three minutes into the warning, the mistake was found. Fortunately, there was someone near—a live person—who could think rationally and correct the mistake.

Not all breakdowns in computers and other systems that guide, if not control, our lives have such immediate and dangerous consequences. Nevertheless, the frustrations they elicit are just as immediate and overwhelming. No one is immune from frustration and the negative emotional backwash it creates.

For over a year, Martin Marty, theologian, scholar, author, and historian, tried to talk to a system, a computer, anybody or anything that would listen to his claim for a $47.90 airline ticket refund. He felt frustrated at every turn. He had followed all the rules for getting the refund, sent follow-up registered letters; but nothing happened in response, not a check or a letter of explanation. Among the whole range of possible problems we humans face, this refund was hardly worth the worry. Nevertheless, for over a year Marty's frustration festered, until it exploded in his national weekly column:

> To The President, The Vice-Presidents in Charge of Refunds, Complaints and Public Relations . . . I write a column. Its readers all have experiences like mine but I own the column and will speak for them. In the name of all fighters against computers, all victims of impersonal and unheeding and inefficient large corporations, let me speak up. . . .
> You may think that you are free to deal with me as insensitively as you no doubt do with thousands of other

people about whom you do not care. But do not forget that my column and I are *religious*. Religion is not all sop and slop and sweetness. It has a hard edge.

Then he delivered the *coup de grâce* with a not-too-subtle slash of Marty wit—a final thrust of the rapier into a speechless, mindless, unfeeling opponent:

> May lice from the ayatollah's beard infect your office.
> May you be caught at rush hour in a traffic jam during an Edsel owners' convention in Dallas. . . .
> May you spend evenings reading and learning history from the story of Chrysler. . . .
> May your motion-discomfort bags be stuck together with bubble gum. . . .
> May the guardian angels watch over your passengers. And may I, someday, forgive.[3]

A short time after publication, Marty received a check with a noncommittal letter from the airline expressing regrets for the delay. Case closed!

Publicly venting frustrations is not an option for most of us, unless we live where there's an "action line" or "hot line" advocate to work on our behalf. Short of taking to the streets in rioting, or holding hostages, most of us have little choice but to muddle through. We would like an answer, a solution—some resolution—but nothing seems to work. We are angry and disappointed. We feel frustrated and alone in our bad days.

When Frustration Has the Best of Us

To live is to be frustrated at times. We feel frustrated when we temporarily lose control of our lives, or when we can't get what we want. Coping with frustration is like catching a greased pig. The harder we try, the more likely the pig will slip away. Frustrations taken one at a time represent momentary irritations in the day. Collectively they spell disaster.

When frustration gets to us, it pushes everything else away. Nothing else matters—not the presidential election, not high inflation, not floods in the South, or even world anarchy. Whatever the frustration, it demands center stage, our undivided attention, and usually gets it.

We can't avoid every frustration that comes along. Many happen just because we are at the wrong place at the wrong time. But we can cope creatively with the unavoidable. Here are some suggestions.

Separate facts from feelings. Anything that is serious enough to describe as a frustration has two major components—the facts of the situation and the feelings it produces. While the feelings are important because they communicate our reaction to the frustration, facts provide a basis for solutions and answers. If we can look at a problem with distance and objectivity, we can often resolve it. But looking at that same problem out of hurt and anger may prevent us from seeing the issue clearly enough to solve it. In a later chapter we will look more carefully at the value and technique of decision-making as an approach to living the bad days.

To distinguish between the facts of a frustration and the feelings it inspires has another benefit. It frees us to work on the frustration rather than become its victim. Frustrations can paralyze us because they seem so big and menacing. Some of us are frustrated easily because we look at a task, feel overwhelmed by its size, and quit before we start.

"How can you find time to write a book?" people ask me. I tell them that if I think "book," I can easily scare myself into doing nothing. But if I think "three pages a day," then I can have a chapter in a week or so, ten chapters in a summer. Behold, a book! Divide the problem into the smallest units possible. This means taking frustrations one at a time and trying to separate the facts of a situation from the feelings. Consequently, you may see the facts differently, or you may feel differently about the problem.

Take time out. Frustration comes from wanting and not getting. It's organizing your day to accomplish certain tasks, and then being interrupted or stopped. It's standing by helplessly while a friend behaves destructively. It's making what you feel is a good decision, only to have it backfire. It's resolving to mow the lawn and then not being able to start the mower. It's running to make the bus only to watch it drive by. It's having a run of bad days with no end in sight. It's feeling stymied, stupid, and helpless. So universal is this kind of trouble that someone invented Murphy's Law to describe it: *If anything can go wrong, it will.* Additions to Murphy's Law include:

1. Nothing is as easy as it looks.
2. Everything takes longer than you think.
3. If there is a possibility of several things going wrong, the one that will cause the most damage will be the one to go wrong.
4. Left to themselves, things tend to go from bad to worse.
5. It is impossible to make anything foolproof because fools are so ingenious.[4]

Sometimes our days become so impossible with frustrations that all we can do is take time out. The purpose is not to deny the problem, but to give it distance. "In stress research," Selye advises, "we have found that, when completion of one particular task becomes impossible, diversion, a voluntary change of activity, is frequently as good as—if not better than—a rest."[5] Relaxation, he says, comes by taking the stress off one system—our nervous system for example—and putting it on our muscles in vigorous exercise; as, for example, when people vigorously start housecleaning to avoid beginning an arduous mental task. Exercise researchers at the University of Wisconsin verify this. Exercise can release many common, everyday tensions of living. Riding a bicycle, jogging, or even taking a brisk walk for at least a half hour may be just enough time out to let a creative idea poke through any struggling, fretting or worrying. A nonexercising, slightly heavy colleague and wit, however, maintains that running is so painful he can't think about anything else.

Do a disappearing act, counsels Wayne Oates in his advice to people under stress.[6] Cover your responsibilities, of course, and let one other person know where you are, but drop out of sight for whatever time it takes to recover. For some it might require being alone; others may go to the city. A few hours of solitude in the library, a shopping trip in another place, a walk in the park, a visit to someone you haven't seen for a while, a hike in the woods, or just sitting on the bank of a stream—all are ways of getting away. The problem may not go away but you may feel a little differently as you come back to it.

Be a student of life instead of its victim. People seem to fall into one of two categories—either they face up to what life presents to them or they feel victimized by "bad luck" or a punishing God. It's what Dr. Eric Berne, the founding father of transactional analysis, describes as playing the "Kick Me" game or "See What You Made Me Do."[7] In each game the person thinks of himself or herself as a victim, asking: "Why does this always happen to me?" According to Berne, we set ourselves up to be a victim of our frustrations. It's a life attitude that comedian Jackie Gleason made famous as "The Poor Soul"—always reacting to situations, rather than taking charge of the moment. To play the victim is to pile frustration upon frustration without taking any initiative to see what can be done to change the situation.

Those of us who are free of physical handicaps have much to learn from people who, through their disabilities, have reached out to life. It's the difference between resenting the handicap and learning how to live with it. The first is a "victim" approach; the second, a learning approach.

To be a learner means that you try to improve and grow from your mistakes and bad days. The next time you're in the middle of an "up-the-wall" frustration, don't ask: "Why does this always happen to me?" Instead, ask: "What have I learned from this?" Be a learner instead of a victim.

Preventing Unnecessary Frustrations

We can't get away from life's stresses and frustrations, but we can prevent unnecessary bad days.

Know what frustrations you can and cannot avoid. Some things happen to us just because we exist—the weather, for instance. We want to go on a picnic and it rains. We plant the garden and it doesn't rain. We slow our car to avoid hitting a cat, and another driver hits us from the rear. An unavoidable frustration. Or, we know that we've had a rough week at work and look forward to the weekend. But a neighbor asks us to help with the neighborhood barbeque. We don't really want to, but we feel obligated and say yes. We feel frustrated and resentful.

An inattentive driver's bumping into our car is a

situation over which we have no control. It's a frustration because it's a needless accident. We happened to be there. But the neighborhood event is an example of a preventable frustration. Only we can make decisions about how we'll use our time. Many of us can't say no to demands, no matter how unnecessary they are. Then we put ourselves into boxes that pressure us with frustration and anger.

The next time a request is made of you, ask:

1. What's being asked of me?
2. Do I really want to do it?

If you must consider the "shoulds" and "oughts" of the situation, think carefully about their impact on your tolerance for frustration. What's the risk in saying yes or no? You don't have to be selfish about it. If you make up your mind to do a few good deeds—for the PTA, the neighborhood association, etc.—twice a year and then plan on them, you won't have to feel guilty about saying no to other requests.

When you say yes or no, mean it. Do you handle your schedule as if you were standing at a buffet table taking everything in sight, filling up on appetizers and desserts? Just as your body does not have unlimited capacity at a buffet table, it rebels at the amount of stress it can take at any one time. Learn your limits, how much sleep you need, the best kind of exercise, your tolerance for feeling pressured, and capacity for frustration.

Do not commit yourself beyond your physical and mental ability to say yes. To agree to every demand upon your time and energy, for whatever reason, is to give priority to everyone's demands before your own. That's a sure way to bring on a bad day.

When you cannot meet all that's expected of you, you

feel frustrated. If you say yes more than no to such demands, then you probably need to reassess priorities. The simple word "no" can be a great frustration-reducer. *For everything you want to do, have a back-up plan.* Dream big dreams, set far-out goals, be clear about what you want. But have Plan B at the ready. This is the back-up when you can't get what you want. If your dreams are off in the clouds, you can frustrate yourself trying to reach them, setting yourself up for failure and disappointment.

Have mind and life-stretching goals, but give yourself a back-up plan that you can still achieve in case the first choice doesn't work out. It's like having two engines on an airplane. If the first one fails, the second one will still keep you in the air.

Since frustration comes when we can't get what we want, having Plan B is a recognition that frustration is normal. Our wants may conflict with what someone else wants, creating frustration. If Plan B is a compromise, so be it. Creative living means day-to-day problem-solving with some of the solutions being worked out as compromises. Dictators know how to handle frustrations—jail or shoot anyone who stands in the way. The rest of us have to find alternatives, since there are not enough jails or bullets to handle a good week's supply of frustrations!

Welcome occasional frustration—it reminds you that you are alive. The next time you are frustrated—in either a large or small dose—don't panic. Resist thinking of it as an aberration that, like lightning, has struck you—a chance happening or a punishment meted out by hostile gods. To feel frustration doesn't mean you've failed or lost control. It means that Plan A isn't working or hasn't developed. It means that you face a problem that has both fact and feelings attached to it. It means that you have the choice of approaching the problem either as a victim or as a learner.

How you approach it is the difference between giving in or living the bad days.

Finally, don't panic if you've tried everything and nothing seems to work. Some problems are like that, and so are many frustrations. If there were easy answers, there would be no frustrations, and life would indeed be dull.

2

Resentment—The Destructive Emotion

Pauline and I took an afternoon drive with friends recently, through the new urban sprawl of a once rural community near Milwaukee, my first parish assignment out of seminary. Past the blue and silver silos that punctuated the landscape like giant exclamation marks, under the scrutiny of curious Guernseys, through new subdivisions, we drove past my first church, standing proudly at the top of a knoll. Suddenly, the years telescoped, and I felt that I had only been away on a long vacation. We looked at the bare spot where our first house had once stood, now nothing but grass where the hand-hewn stone thresholds once lay. As we drove by, brightly dressed people streamed into the little chapel for a wedding. I was tempted to stop, but we drove on, turning off the highway and onto the gravel path that wound through the township cemetery.

I had been there many times for funerals and had marveled at the care with which the old sexton staked out each new grave while his grandson on winter days tried to thaw the frozen sod with charcoal. How would they ever get through the frost in time for the service? There wasn't much that was fancy about country cemeteries—not like their big-city cousins. Country gravediggers didn't try to hide the reddish-brown diggings with false grass. People in that first parish accepted dirt as a part of dying.

We took our friends into the cemetery, a gallery of local history, pointing out Scottish, Irish, and Welsh names on old headstones. Each name teased out a memory and a story for my captive audience. One name surprised me—Charles M———, born 1908, died 1968. I remembered him as a young man. I pondered his death—and life—thinking back twenty years when I knew him to be embittered and resentful.

The reason was no secret. People said that before the Great Depression, his father, then the church's treasurer, attempted a worthy, but ill-advised, gesture. He invested congregational funds in stocks that evaporated as the banks closed. Although his father repaid the debt, young Charles felt he inherited the blame. Nevertheless, he continued to live and farm in the community. Some thought that a new pastor might break down his resentment with youthful enthusiasm and evangelical zeal. I called occasionally, but he never let me get close to him. We usually chatted near the barn. I was never invited in. He was pleasant enough, but I couldn't bring myself to probe his old hurts. We talked about the weather, the price of milk, and whatever else masked my real reason for being there. It is ironic that in death he now lies forever among those he most resented.

What power resentment can hold over us, increasing in its intensity with each day it goes unresolved. It's as if we have a miniature volcano within. From a distance, the look is benign, even tranquil, but inside we're boiling, always under pressure and unpredictable. Consider the potential for destruction of the spirit when resentment has been boiling five, ten, or more years.

I thought of Charles, and I pitied him. But standing at

his grave, I remembered my own fury and pain I thought I had forgotten, but had not entirely forgiven. For a moment, Charles and I had become brothers in spirit, joined together with everyone who has harbored resentment for past hurts. I shuddered and rejoined my friends.

Nothing stimulates memory and uncovers an old and unresolved anger like a resentment whose time has come. We all have ghosts that haunt us from the past—old hurts, disappointments, and conflicts hidden away in yellowed letters, school yearbooks, and other artifacts of years gone by.

Resentment is an anger that has burrowed underground like a mole. You can't see the rascal, but you can trace its destructiveness as it plows up the lawn you've so carefully groomed. With resentment, all it takes is some memory to bring it to consciousness.

Resentment creates bad days because we invest so much in trying to keep the lid on our anger. If we really feel steamed about something (as we rightly express it), we can go from zero pressure to over 500 lbs. per square inch within a short time. The target can be a friend, a spouse, a child, a neighbor, a co-worker—even the person who promised to fix the vacuum cleaner. It doesn't make much difference who it is. It can be anyone who makes us feel trapped or has put an excessive or unreasonable demand upon us.

Anger, and even hostility, are normal responses to everyday irritations and frustrations between people who work or live together. The history of anger, says Leo Madow, professor at the Medical College of Pennsylvania, is the history of Humankind.[1] However, anger is such a powerful emotion that many of us have invented ways to hide it or get around it. Unfortunately we aren't able to do either, but we vigorously pursue the illusion by putting the lid of resentment on to push down the anger. A resentful day can quickly turn the bloom of a good mood into a dull ache that desolates the human spirit. We may allow minor explosions to take some of the pressure off and help us feel better, but the resentment keeps building the pressure up. And all of our bodily systems have to bear the stress.

Recognizing Signs of Resentment

Resentment gives off many warnings. Give yourself the following test to see if you recognize any of them. The situation is a real problem that was reported recently in a national secretaries' journal. Read it through carefully, and then I'll ask you about it. Your response to my questions may tell you something about how you handle your own resentments.

Starting time at our office is 8:00 A.M. Unfortunately, my co-worker, Jan, makes it a daily practice to arrive at any time between 8:15 and 8:30 A.M. Her absence is not really noticeable to anyone as I cover for her by answering phones and doing any rush jobs that need to be done. This means that any small jobs of my own, such as photocopying and distributing of mail have to wait until Jan gets in (which is also the same time things begin to get hectic around the office, and is another situation which makes it difficult for me to get away from my desk).

The problem of her daily late arrival has been discussed with Jan several times by her supervisor, with our staff psychologist, and myself. But none of these discussions has made any difference.

I'm at the end of my rope, and am beginning to feel very bitter toward Jan. I cannot help feeling cheated, knowing that it has been over a year now since I've been working with Jan, and she still has not been able to solve this problem. I've tried to work my own schedule around hers, trying to get my photocopying and distributing work done at night, and saving typing jobs for first thing in the morning. I've also come in early to do important photocopying, knowing that if I wait until 8:00, the job will not get done on time. This system works, but is it really fair to me?

Please tell me what to do before I "blow my stack," and end up losing a relatively good working relationship with her.

P.S. It is now 9:15 A.M. and I'm still waiting for her to come in! Help!

JMK, Detroit[2]

Please jot down on a scrap of paper any memories, feelings, and initials of people and experiences of your own that come to mind as you read JMK's story. How long have these memories—or resentments—been with you?

Don't read any farther until you have attempted one more experiment with this true example. See if you can outline one, two, or three steps for resolving the problem if you were in JMK's position. Put down what you *really* feel, not what you think you *ought* to say or do. As a final activity, note the risks or pay-offs of the behavior you have indicated. Just to make this a bit more difficult, let me offer one more complication: if you go to the supervisor and he or she decides to do nothing about the problem, what are your alternatives? Will any of these lead to an unresolved resentment? At what cost to you?

Now, look at some ways you might have chosen to cope with the problem. Each of the following techniques is commonly used to handle resentments. They, indeed, are clear signs of unresolved anger.

Teasing with a biting edge. I invite teasing and I like to tease. Among those I know and respect, I'll take every opportunity to place a well-sharpened barb. This game of intimacy continues only if my partner plays. This means that he or she has the right to shoot barbs at me. But teasing can be destructive between friends when it is motivated by resentment rather than playfulness. It's a little like that childhood amusement in which one person slaps the other's wrist and the other slaps back. Enthusiasm of one or both players frequently ruins the game and one or the other has to stop it.

Friendly teasing can help friends laugh at themselves, their foibles, and life's frustrations. But it has to affirm, not tear down. Destructive teasing can cause resentment and it's also a sign of hidden resentment.

Distancing. Resentment that keeps on long after the precipitating event or situation can cause distance, rather than closeness in a relationship. Look for the signs, like curtness or short, crisp answers to questions. When we are resentful, a chill characterizes the interaction as we respond with brief answers and general stiffness. The ways we sit, walk, or stare out the window in the presence of the person we resent are clues.

Curtness may lead to completely ignoring people we resent, treating them as if they did not exist. Therapist and author Adelaide Bry describes this as "stuffing" anger: "But the idea of doing something about it, expressing it in some way, any way, is so frightening in terms of the way others might respond, that despite their seething insides, they mask their feelings, usually by adopting a grin-and-bear-it 'What do I care?' attitude."[3] The truth is that most stuffers do care, but haven't the courage to deal directly with their resentment.

If your resentment centers on someone you live or work with on a day-to-day basis, and there's no way to get away from that person, you may use sabotage to show your hidden anger. "Sabotage is a sneaky way to get one's anger message across," says Adelaide Bry, "not so much because the Saboteur is necessarily such a sneaky person, but because the anger is expressed so deviously and in such 'small' ways."⁴ At one extreme, the Saboteur snips away at self-esteem; and at the other, the object is to tear down or subvert the other's ideas or suggestions. The snipping may be so slight that it goes by unnoticed. But collectively, it adds up to one huge put-down. Using the secretary's example, JMK might have said to Jan: "Oh, you're not wearing that again, are you?" after many "minor" veiled comments about Jan's lateness. Such a comment probably communicates resentment more than a judgment about dress.

Distancing in its extreme—the last resort—is to remove the cause of the anger. This means either taking the other person out of the situation or withdrawing yourself. By putting the object of anger out of sight, we think we can stay our anger. It doesn't work that way for me, however—the resentment grows as time passes. Distancing causes people to settle for separate bedrooms, move to other places, bury themselves in excessive work or other activities. And still the resentment grinds on. Withdrawing offers only a temporary respite from the pain. I'm always amazed, as I look into the mirror, how creative we humans can be at avoiding being direct and open with one another—we'd rather lick our festering wounds for twenty years in private, than suffer a brief and decisive confrontation to get at the problem.

Fault-finding. People have a right and a responsibility to talk with each other about all kinds of issues. Criticism can be a useful communication tool to identify problems and suggest solutions. But fault-finding for the purpose of inflicting hurt is a weapon of the resentful. It is not interested in solutions, only in punishment. To tell the difference between hurting someone and giving honest criticism, notice what's being talked about. If the intention is to hurt the other person (to punish), then the focus will be on the person. But if the intention is to be helpful, then the criticism will be objective and focused on behavior.

The Cost of Resenting

Like the steam and ash of a volcano that's about to blow, anger, as a form of energy, must surface somewhere. "Unrecognized anger," Madow says, "can contribute to many physical disabilities, and its recognition may help to alleviate a significant portion of the problem."[5] Some of the symptoms he lists are headaches, gastrointestinal disorders, respiratory disorders, skin disorders, genito-urinary disorders, arthritis, disabilities of the nervous system, and circulatory problems. In addition, there seems to be a close link between buried anger and depression. If any of these symptoms persists, the doctor advises, consult a psychologically oriented physician.

If you have ever been depressed, you know how terrible it feels. It numbs, immobilizes, makes you feel hopeless. You feel sad when all signs say you should be happy. You grieve, but know not why or for whom. You cry, but tears bring no relief. You feel imprisoned in a grayness that is without beginning or end. Acute event-specific sad-ness—like a death or sudden loss—has a beginning and an end. Crying makes you feel better. The depressed person, on the other hand, sees the clouds and wonders if the sun will ever shine again.

Depression can be a serious emotional disturbance, and in severe instances it must be treated with both therapy and medication. However, most minor attacks of "the blues" are normal reactions to stresses around us. They may be related to vague feelings of unhappiness at not being able to express anger at someone important, says

Rolland Parker, a New York psychologist. The result is resentment that turns inward and sets us up for a bad day.[6]

Preventing and Coping With Resentments

Ideally, the best way to handle resentment is to prevent it in the first place. But that's easier said than done. We'd have to find some way to keep ourselves from being angry and hurt, but because that's usually impossible, we have to deal with our distress right at the time. Anger is a natural human emotion, often as expressive of our caring as it is of our contempt.

Resentment is fermenting anger. It has been allowed to sour over a long time. Then, when it does come out as resentment, it really stings.

If you feel resentful, you need to ask:

1. How can I prevent unnecessary resentment?
2. What can I do when I feel resentful?

The key to preventing resentment is nothing magic, merely good common sense for effective interpersonal communication. First, be alert to the "resentment signs" in your own behavior. If you find yourself delivering "humorous" barbs (teasing) without smiling and with the intent to hurt, then be alert to possible hostility. If you engage in any of the distancing behavior previously mentioned, look for hidden resentment. The same goes for fault-finding or nit-picking criticism.

Second, listen to what your body may be trying to tell you—by headache, nervousness, rapid pulse, or other physical symptoms.

Third, try to deal with the resentments openly and directly. Jesus said, "If you are bringing your offering to the altar and there remember that your brother has something against you, leave your offering there before the altar, go and be reconciled with your brother first" (Matt. 5:24). Concentrate on how to work out the problem at issue, rather than finding fault.

Fourth, be prepared to accept reality. You may find that your hurt makes confrontation impossible. Emotionally, we're sometimes unable to deal directly with situations until we've taken time out—allowed a little space for cooling off our feelings so good judgment can prevail. Give yourself this time and space, recognizing that the price to pay might be a few bad days. Also, the other person may reject your overtures, leaving you more frustrated.

When we are unable to prevent or avoid resentment, then we have to apply other measures to help us through the inevitable rocky times. Keep firmly in mind that although you may feel momentarily out of control, the very fact that you are feeling (and aware of the pain) means that you are alive and you care.

Allow yourself to feel, to daydream, and to be openly angry—without pushing the anger down, denying its existence, or exploding on some other target. Some psychologists suggest shouting out an open window, beating pillows, or some other action to diffuse pent-up energy. I've found jogging, (bicycling, swimming, tennis, walking, housecleaning—anything that's physically exerting) to be helpful. By taking care of yourself you are providing a safety vent for pressure that would otherwise be destructive.

Physical exercise may not dissolve the problem, but it may change how you view it, as well as how you see yourself. Another helpful step may be to talk with a friend or counselor who can help you sort out the issues. Also, remember that reaching for alcohol or prescription drugs only delays the search for solutions.

Now that you have looked at some early signs of resentment, its potential cost to health and relationships, and how you might either prevent or cope with hidden anger, reread the case example of JMK's complaint toward Jan. What would you advise JMK to do?

Consider these options. JMK could do nothing and let the resentment build, with possible untoward conseqences. JMK could insist that management solve the problem with severe disciplinary action. Or JMK could continue to pursue the problem directly with Jan in the hope of working out a solution. There may be circumstances in Jan's personal life that contribute to her lateness. Nevertheless, JMK will have to take the initiative by speaking plainly and caringly to Jan. Jan must be made aware of how her behavior affects her co-workers. Hopefully she will change, or a compromise can be worked out.

If the problem can't be worked out with Jan, then JMK may have to consider whether she wants to continue in that particular job or pursue her complaint with management.

Anger is a basic human emotion, as JMK knows only too well. Most of us would prefer to deny it, avoid it, or otherwise go around it, rather than confront it head-on. Yet, the head-on approach—before the anger has had a chance to smolder too long—can save us some unnecessary bad days.

3

Threats—The Things That Scare Us

The late Alfred Hitchcock, film director, was a master at scaring people. The suspense he created was as unbearable as the danger itself. With just the right camera angles and tight direction, Hitchcock brought people to the edge of their seats in what was probably his scariest film—*Psycho*. The shower-murder scene itself was a heart-stopper, although the British-born director took great care to show no actual details of violence. We never see the knife touch the woman's flesh. Cinematographic illusion seduces the audience into believing the scene was shot in color. It was actually filmed in black and white.

In *North by Northwest* (some say his best American film), Hitchcock has Cary Grant, a business executive mistaken for a secret agent, trying to outrun a crop-dusting plane chasing after him in an Indiana cornfield. The audience runs breathlessly alongside the hero, fear dogging each step. Cary Grant escapes and so do we.[1]

In both pictures, the danger is fake, but the fear is real. It's artificial terror that makes us want to fight or run. It is indeed an irony that in our time—already dubbed the age of anxiety—people willingly spend millions of dollars to buy fear in a theater, and many times that amount trying to rid themselves of the normal fears that produce bad days.

In this chapter we'll look at how we handle threats— worry, anxiety, and fear—and how we can cope with these feelings.

Living Is Handling Threats

Friends called the other night to tell us about their trip to Ireland, to bring us up to date on their family, to ask us how we were, and to tell us that the doctors had found cancer cells in Judy's breast. Pauline stammered out one of those what-can-you-say-at-a-time-like-this responses, and I dusted off something from past ministerial days. The threat to our friend had shaken our own security. Growing up, we think people live forever, and really big crises only happen to people out there somewhere, people we don't know.

Living is handling threats—the obvious physical ones tied to health and aging, and the psychological threats that come with job loss, a child in trouble, parents growing older, alcoholism or drug abuse in the family, or a host of other worries. There are also spiritual threats that have to do with values and goals—trying to answer the question, "Does my life have purpose and meaning?"

Threats bring on bad days because they upset our peace and serenity, as we shall explore in the next section.

Reacting to Threats

Worry. The first level, the slow burn, of being scared is worry. Worry, a simmering, under-the-surface fear, is like a run of rainy days on a vacation. The bad weather doesn't send you packing home, but it is enough to drain any enthusiasm you had. Worry is like an ache that won't quit. It's not enough to make you sick, but just enough that you don't feel well.

Some people are occasional worriers; others make it a career. Homer R——— was a career worrier and a good fisherman. This was an unbeatable combination on days when fishing was off. What entertainment the fish didn't produce, Homer's worrying did.

One calm summer evening, Homer, Bill, and I put our boat into a kettle-moraine lake in south central Wisconsin. No sooner had we gotten under way than Homer, who worried for all of us, began to fret about the dangers of fishing from a boat. First, he worried about whether the boat would sink, and then he worried about someone's getting hit with a misdirected cast. As we moved through a beautiful Pine Lake sunset, the boat stayed afloat, but one of Bill's casts went awry and hooked Homer superficially in the ear—of all people to have such an accident! Bill and I could barely contain our laughter while Homer worried about how he would look with "only half an ear." He was convinced that Bill was about to surgically remove his ear right there in the boat. With a little antiseptic and a band-aid, the emergency passed and we were back at the disappointing task of trying to catch fish. At sundown, we headed back to the boat landing.

Before the night was over, we had to contend with another of Homer's worries. Backing the boat trailer hitched to an old Ford station wagon down the steep embankment toward the landing, he shouted out the window, "What if the brakes fail and I go into the lake?" The scene was comical. There was Homer, inching that old car and trailer down a steep incline, while Bill and I teased him with "how cold the water was" and "how the brakes were slipping."

The brakes held. The boat securely tied on the trailer, we

headed home. But Homer already had a head start on his next worry—something about misplacing the flashlight and "what if" the trailer unhooked before we got home.

Anxiety. While some people worry about a particular event or situation, others often feel upset without any specific cause. This "nervousness" or nameless fear is anxiety. Anxiety, to some degree, is a normal element in living.

Anxiety can be helpful as well as destructive. Too little leads to boredom, apathy, or carelessness. Too much neurotic anxiety tends to make people pull back from all risks and feel paralyzed. The right amount of anxiety, one physician writes, "alerts us, buoys us, and motivates us." On the other hand, too much is like that electronic auditory effect—called "white noise"—that's introduced into public buildings to drown out unwanted sounds. The right amount filters out extraneous, unwanted sounds. Too much makes people tense and nervous.

According to government reports, Americans suffer from too much anxiety. Tranquilizer and anti-anxiety agents are the most prescribed medications in our country. In 1978, the Food and Drug Administration reported that 2.5 billion Valium tablets were sold; just one brand of the 68 million individual prescriptions written for all benzodiazepines. The press reported an FDA Commissoner's warning: "These drugs were not intended merely to deal with normal anxiety."

Psychiatrist Rollo May gives an example of what he believes to be normal anxiety—standing up before a group to talk, an event that scares many of us. He describes how he tried to rid himself of the perspiring hands, dry mouth, and rapid pulse—and the price he had to pay for inner peace.

One day, tired of enduring this tension, which seemed so unnecessary, and with the help of a strong resolve, I proceeded to condition myself out of the anxiety. That evening I was perfectly relaxed and free from tension when I mounted the platform. But I made a poor speech. Missing were the tension, the sense of challenge, the zest of the race horse at the starting gate—those states of mind and body in which normal anxiety expresses itself.[2]

Such anxiety is essential to the human condition, the psychiatrist maintains. It is "Being affirming itself against Nonbeing," which is another way of saying that being alive produces a certain amount of anxiety.

Anxiety is the human spirit in contest against a depersonalized, robotlike destiny—a struggle between meaning and meaninglessness.

Anxiety not only warns us of impending meaninglessness in our lives, but it's the product of living without purpose and meaning. In the right balance, anxiety pushes us to life's creative edge; too much paralyzes. Our task is to distinguish the helpful anxiety from the hurtful—not an easy assignment for an aspirin-minded, tranquilizer-saturated culture.

Fear. Now a look at near-panic fear, the third and most severe fight/flight response to real and imagined threats. Fear can wallop us with a two-fisted punch. The first is an automatic reaction to danger. It catches us off guard. But adrenalin quickly stirs the body and psyche into action. Then comes the second punch, pushing us to the edge of panic. It's fear that says, "Oh, my goodness, what if. . . ." What if I faint in this crowd? What if Mother doesn't get well? What if I have cancer? What if it's a heart attack? It's the Oh-my-goodness-what-ifs that compound normal, rational fear into irrational and difficult-to-cope-with panic. Second-punch fears make us feel as gray as paste. We sweat and our hearts pound.

Confronting Our Fears

What can we do about the worries, anxieties, and panic-level fears that precipitate bad days and rob us of joy? One obvious solution would be to eliminate the things that threaten us, thereby doing away with the yucky feelings that characterize the bad days. But then life would be sterile, like the germ-free bubble for people born without normal immune systems. Every contact with the world would become a major threat to life. Every expression of love—each hug and kiss—would have to be filtered through the paraphernalia of security: pumped-in oxygen, plastic tubing, rubber gloves to prevent any contact with normal bacteria. The smallest mistake could be fatal.

I've known people who have tried to live in a psychologically sterile bubble. They shriveled. I once tried it and nearly made myself sick. Some seem to survive on half-living, never risking too much, rarely venturing far from the safety of the known and the guaranteed.

Don't you want something more out of life? Do you want to live inside a sterile plexiglass bubble, or behind a barbed wire fence, or inside a moated fortress? I prefer a style of life that's similar to fishing for bass or trout. First of all, you go where there's some chance for success, and then you cast out your line and hope to be surprised. If the first cast doesn't reel home a fish, then you try a second, and a third, or more. If there's still no action, you move to another spot. The serious fisherman doesn't sit on the bank and wait for a strike. Reaching out to life is like fishing—the successes are often found where there is the best chance of getting snagged. But the prize is usually worth the minor aggravations. For example, reaching out to a new friend is one of life's prizes, but we risk snagging a rejection. In going after a particular job, we may have to cast our lines into the tangled brush of uncertainty. We may reel in nothing more than a "Don't call us, we'll call you," or we may be surprised and land the job.

Whatever the risk or threat, we know the now-familiar feelings that go along with it—worry, anxiety, and fear. If we can't avoid life's threats, we can find a way to cope with the fears that are so distressing. Here are some suggestions.

When feeling upset, identify the threat. "Being able to accept and identify a wide range of our experiences defuses them and takes the threat out of them," says psychologist Eugene Kennedy. "We do not end up feeling that we are living with an attic filled with bats. We will understand that the human situation is the only one in which we can exist and that we have to accept and label correctly all aspects of our experience to know ourselves and take effective charge of our behavior."[3] To label a threat correctly helps us with the emotions that come with it. Then feeling bad doesn't take us by surprise. Sure, there will be a bad day or two, but at least we know what's behind it—and that makes the feelings easier to take. We can accept them as a normal, natural response to a threat.

Be aware of knock-down, "second-punch" fears. Like the fighter's one-two punch, the first jab knocks you off guard, while the second punch knocks you out. Knowing what's coming, more than strength, fends off this kind of assault. Remember that the first fear comes automatically in response to a danger. If that first fear takes you by surprise, then the second-punch fear can add to your pain. And the two fears together feel like one massive wallop on the head.

"Must you let these physical feelings hold such terror?" writes Australian physician Claire Weekes. "Must you let them, horrible though they may be, spoil your life when the way to calm them is within your own power?" She tells us what most alert doctors already know and tell their patients, *"You are bluffed by physical feelings of no great medical significance."*[4]

Heading off second-punch fears is not easy, but it is possible. Instead of tensing, practice acceptance, even as you feel fearful. You've probably been in this situation before. Say to yourself, "I've lived through this once; I'll do it again. It is not pleasant, but I'll do it." That's the first step toward acceptance.

For example, if you become fearful in a crowd—at the supermarket, in a theater, or wherever large numbers of people gather—resist running for the nearest exit. Running out may make you feel better temporarily, but you are still at the mercy of your fear. Practice seeing the panic through, counsels Dr. Weekes. You will feel shaky at first, but you will also begin to experience your own strength. Victory is not to be found in some cheap, easy remedy, but in the struggle of facing up to a fear and working through it.

Do not worry about tomorrow; tomorrow will take care of itself. This advice is more than two thousand years old. That Jesus said it at all indicates that worrying about tomorrow is an age-old preoccupation—one that keeps us from fully appreciating today. Fear adds nothing. It detracts. It consumes our energy and takes from today. Nevertheless, we do worry about tomorrow. That seems to be our nature—a dark shadow of the spirit through which we filter our days.

Pundit Andy Rooney has figured out that if we live eighty years, that gives us 29,220 days. "Most of us," he says, "live at half speed most of the time and we lose a lot of good living that way. We goof off or don't have a plan or, for one reason or another, don't do much with many of our days."[5] And many of those days we waste by worrying about tomorrow, which the Bible says will take care of itself. Much of what we fear about tomorrow never happens. We've worried for nothing. We've wasted our energy, and we've put ourselves through bad days needlessly.

To take today as it comes—not worrying about tomorrow—is to savor today's joy as well as today's sorrow. Sure, we will occasionally feel the blahs, sweaty palms, and dry mouth. But we will also feel the exhilaration of being alive and "all together" some days too. To take today as it comes means that we accept ourselves—our feelings, our failures, our successes—knowing that today's pain or joy will help us for tomorrow. We can only experience success by daring to risk defeat, defying the fear of failure, and allowing ourselves to strive for less than absolute perfection.

4

Loneliness—An Emptiness Within

Recently, thirty people came to a workshop in northern Wisconsin on "living with loneliness." Roger Williams, an associate, and I were leading it. He asked the group, "How have you experienced loneliness?" Here are some of their answers:

"When you no longer feel needed."

"When your family is gone and you remember the wonderful times when you were together—especially the holidays."

"When you don't hear from your family."

"When you are in a strange environment."

"When a relationship changes or terminates through illness or death."

"When you feel unwanted."

Throughout the day people talked about their loneliness—the young wife of an alcoholic, an aging widow, a recently retired salesman, a Chicago schoolteacher who had moved north to escape the obsessions of the city, a woman whose husband's health had failed. As members of the group exchanged information about themselves and discovered mutual interests, they exchanged telephone numbers and promised they would call after the program.

Most began to reach out to one another; except Ada, an elderly woman who sat apart from the rest of the group. She listened intently. Growing increasingly impatient, she bluntly interrupted, "Tell me how not be lonely!" Again in the afternoon session her impatience overcame shyness, and she asked the question again, "Tell me how to make friends!" All of us could feel the intensity of Ada's pain—both its reality and its unreality. She hurt, but she also wanted some magic to take it away. Even as two or three people offered to take her telephone number and call her, she seemed bewildered—unable to recognize even the magic of that unsolicited reaching out to her. Would Ada accept these friendship initiatives? Would she call back? Roger and I talked about Ada and the others as we drove back to Madison. As darkness closed in during the five-hour trip and we looked for a warm, cozy place to have dinner, I realized that Ada had spoken not only for herself, for the group, but also for me.

There is no doubt that loneliness—along with frustration, resentment, and threats—is a source of bad days. But how can we cope with loneliness? In this chapter, I'll try to respond to Ada's concern, which troubles all of us now and again.

The Experience of Loneliness

I was first aware of my own loneliness when I left home for college. I was lonely. Frightened by this feeling, I tried to escape with long walks through the narrow, gray streets of Lexington's black community, which bordered the college and backed up to Ewing Hall where I had a room. Feeling disconnected from the closeness of a loving family, I tasted the bittersweetness of manhood and independence, but deep inside I still felt like a little boy.

Dimly lighted windows shone from unpainted, weathered houses of that southern ghetto community, touching the bleak interior of my own sad spirit. There was something magnetic about those orange splashes of color along Upper Street.

That was thirty years ago, and I am still moved by orange windows in the night.

The little houses of the black community abutted against the back yards of stately, columned mansions of the "Old South." Those little houses seemed to have people around and in them; the big mansions looked cold and distant in comparison. Tourists came to Kentucky to see the mansions of Confederate history, but I searched out those orange windows in the night shining like beacons out of the deepening shadows of evening.

I couldn't see inside the windows with drawn shades, but I imagined people eating dinner together and mothers tucking their children into bed, assuring them that everything would be all right.

After all these years, orange windows still tug at me on late night drives through Wisconsin's sand country and farmland. It doesn't take much to tease out the memories—a faded billboard, the familiar call of the meadowlark, or the blues of a rejected lover on the radio. And I look for the twinkling orange lights of passing farmhouses, barns, or rural villages that remind me that people are near, and I am not really alone.

I recently met a woman I'll call Barbara who was painfully going it alone for the second time, thirty-seven years old, and recently widowed, off to visit friends. We had been stranded earlier that day in Alabama with an unexpected flight cancellation, and we hitched a ride for the seventy miles to Birmingham with a state mental health official, whom I had met the evening before.

During the hour's trip over Interstate 59, the three of us

cautiously initiated the usual "hello, how are you?" chit-chat. Barbara, quiet for a few moments after this opening round of introductions, took the first risk and asked, "What do you know about the widow-to-widow program?"

Our driver offered a few suggestions and I bluntly asked, "Are you . . .?"

"Nearly six months," she interrupted, and continued to press for advice about starting a chapter. We arrived at the airport and unloaded our bags. I asked Barbara if she would mind talking more about her first days of being alone. Over coffee her eyes moistened slightly as she described how her husband, out on an errand, had died when his car skidded and crashed.

"What a beautiful life we had together," she said. "I feel like I'm starting all over again."

"What about loneliness?" I asked, sensing she wanted to talk about it. I was also aware that I was projecting a bit of my own feelings into the interview.

"Evenings and weekends are really downers," she replied. "What I miss most is being with men and children. I miss being in a family." She hesitated while the server poured a fresh cup of coffee. "I'm constantly being asked to lunch by my friends, but never over to dinner or out for the weekend."

As her plane was called, Barbara shook my hand and left. Sitting over a half cup of cold coffee I pondered what she had told me. I thought about orange windows in the night and wondered where Barbara would find her comfort.

Everyone, to some extent, lives with loneliness or the fear of it. The seeds of our separateness and the dread of being cut off from life's simplest pleasures and from people we love lie deep within the furrows of the soul. The act of dying is the one final experience of life that we must go through alone, and the thought can be terrifying.

Loneliness is a part of being human. Author Thomas Wolfe describes it as "far from being a rare and curious phenomenon, peculiar to myself." Rather it is a point of acute awareness of the self, bringing a person deeply in touch with his or her own existence and in touch with others. Harold Blake Walker, writing in the *Chicago Tribune,* says that loneliness is the lonely "I" rubbing against another lonely "I" so that the isolated "I's" become "we."[1]

What brings on loneliness?

Robert Weiss, dubbed the "Father of Loneliness Research," believes that loneliness is a signal that our attachment system is in trouble. He says people need (1) a sense of attachment (provided by a lover or spouse), and (2) a sense of community that comes with a network of friends who share concerns and interests. When one or both of these is interrupted, he contends, the result may be loneliness. Weiss believes that the only real cure for loneliness is to replace the missing provision—for example, a new love for those recently widowed or separated.[2]

But for many people in our society, a new love is not a possibility. They are people who have experienced what I call "circumstantial celibacy." They have been cut off from an intimate relationship by the circumstances of illness, death, or separation. Or other circumstances in their lives have prevented an intimate relationship. They didn't ask for these circumstances; this was how life came to them. Friendships with the opposite sex, at best, are constrained by the taboos and limitations of a society that is embarrassed by genuine intimacy.

After my father died twenty-two years ago, my mother was treated for acute depression. She recovered enough to teach school until age seventy. But she never really came to terms with her loneliness. I suspected this—she put out enough clues. However, it wasn't until I was going through her papers after she died that I knew for sure. There, in the midst of her correspondence, were computer printouts from a dating service she had joined. There were names with check marks in front of them, and others crossed out. No clues existed as to the meaning of those marks. That mystery had also died. Mother desperately wanted to be close to another man after Dad's death at age fifty-six, but opportunity diminished as she grew older. She had to settle for imaginary loves, taking long trips to exotic places looking for her own "fantasy island" and "love boat." Many people in our country live in that kind of loneliness and fantasy.

The question is not, Will loneliness strike? but, When? One national study reported that, within any period of several weeks, more than a quarter of all American adults feel painfully lonely, and that the incidence among adolescents is considerably higher.[3]

Wisconsin native Terri Schultz, who has written a poignant personal account of her lifelong battle with loneliness, says, "We can understand loneliness in the hospital, loneliness on a business trip, even loneliness in a crowd, but it is the one thing in life that we do not expect when everything is going right."[4]

One of the first to investigate loneliness, Clark Moustakas admitted that he had lived his loneliness without being aware of it:

> I began to see that in the deepest experiences the human being can know—the birth of a baby, the prolonged illness or death of a loved relative, the loss of a job, the creation of a poem, a painting, a symphony, the grief of a fire, a flood, an accident—each in its own way touches upon the roots of

loneliness. In each of these experiences, in the end, we must go alone.[5]

"All love leads to suffering," he says. "If we did not care for others in a deep and fundamental way, we would not experience grief when they are troubled or disturbed, when they face tragedy or misfortune, when they are ill and dying." It is the pain of loneliness, driving the sun behind the clouds and making our days gray and gloomy, that also expands our capacity to reach out to others while we learn to love the stranger within ourselves.

Just as we humans have the capacity to love, so we have the capacity for loneliness, regardless of whether we live alone or with someone else. The issue is not preventing or avoiding loneliness so much as learning to live with it. That's the conclusion of Moustakas, Schultz, and others. Says Moustakas: "Loneliness is as much a reality of life as night and rain and thunder, and it can be lived creatively, as any other experience . . . for where there is loneliness there is also sensitivity, and where there is sensitivity, there is awareness and recognition and promise."

Terri Schultz agrees: "Living alone makes you see that the great irony of loneliness is that it has nothing to do with how other people feel about you, but with how you feel about yourself."[6]

Giving up the practice of law in New York City to work with Navajos in Arizona, Carolyn Slaby chose to live sixty miles from the nearest town, battling both loneliness and boredom. "I gradually got rid of my fear and learned to accept aloneness and loneliness," she said. "I learned to allow myself to feel loneliness as much as I allow myself to feel happiness and joy."[7]

The old feelings still come back to haunt her, says the young lawyer. She admits to still being terribly lonely, "about four times a year," but she has discovered that she can survive and overcome, bouncing back with resilience because of what she has experienced.

Living with Loneliness

We can't avoid loneliness; we can only learn how to live with it. It's not easy, as one divorced mother describes: "Phones, kids, people, all kinds of action going on. But come 8 P.M. everybody's in bed, and there's this dead silence. Like the whole world has just come to an end."[8]
Loneliness is the feeling that the whole world has stopped. It's the feeling that comes when a spouse or lover has died or left us, or the last child has left home. It's lying in the hospital in the middle of the night before surgery, after family and friends have left. It's being alone during a holiday or on business in a strange city. The empty feeling settles in the pit of the stomach. Everyone says we'll get over it—that it takes time—but it persists. We ask, "What's missing from my life?" hoping that some new friend, or passion, or expensive purchase will fill the void.

The question is not "how to avoid or prevent loneliness" but "how can we live with it as an everyday reality or potentiality?" The question goes beyond whether a person is single or married, living alone or in a community. According to Clark Moustakas, "to love is to be lonely."

To love someone means you must also open yourself to that person's moving away, terminating the friendship, or dying. All love carries the threat of separation or change. And that means pain—the hurt and fear you feel on bad days. Yet, when loneliness touches off a bad day or two, you need not despair. Sure it hurts. But it means that you still have the capacity to love and to feel the absence of the person you care deeply about. It means that, though you feel the pain, you also have the strength to reach for today. To be alive is to have lonely times. That is a reality that Ada had not accepted. It's difficult to accept pain as a natural response to even ordinary life events. There's no way that we can duck around these hurts, but we can learn to live through them. Living is active, not passive. Living requires taking a positive, even risky step out into the day's unknown—without any guarantees of success. Living means reaching out to others—not waiting for miracles or magic. Living means creating our own magic by taking the first step—any step—in facing up to our loneliness. We may not do much to prevent loneliness, but we can keep it from taking us by surprise and knocking us off our feet. Here are some suggestions:

Know what makes you lonely so it doesn't defeat you. All of us have places, things, times of the day and year that call up memories, regrets, and feelings. These are symbols that have meaning beyond themselves. For instance, a particular tree in your yard may be more than just a tree because you sat long hours in its branches as a child. Or it was planted by a favorite uncle. Or maybe under that tree you fell in love. Or you sat under it on Sunday afternoons talking with relatives or listening to the football game. All kinds of symbols fill our lives, reminding us of the past, of happy times, of people who once loved us. Holidays can be particularly rough for people who are alone as they grow older. At Christmas, the carols, candles, shopping, and baking are like voices from the past. To be around these symbols reminds us of the distance between where we have been and where we are now. It increases our sense of isolation. We sense the nearness of death's coldness and desolation.

The Psalms from the Bible are filled with symbols that point to truths beyond their everyday common meanings. "We are like grass," says the Psalmist, "sprouting and

flowering in the morning, withered and dry before dusk"
(Psalm 90). Every time I cut my grass, I think about how
someday this pleasure (I really enjoy it) will disappear. I
like to walk on grass, feel it in my hands, smell it freshly
cut. Even the sound of an old rickety power mower is a
symbol that I listen for in the spring. I never feel quite so
much alive as when I'm cutting grass, nor as lonely as
when I realize the truth of the psalmist's words.

How does awareness of symbols—the things that make
us feel joy or sadness—help us through bad days caused
by loneliness? If we know when, where, and how we feel
lonely, we can take a positive step toward limiting our
vulnerability. We can't avoid loneliness entirely, but we
can learn to face it creatively. If we know that a holiday
makes us feel miserable when we are alone, we can plan
now to find and invite another lonely person to spend it
with us. Instead of waiting to be asked, ask! If you don't
know who to ask, speak with your minister, rabbi, or
priest. Many communities have groups that reach out to
people who are alone on holidays. Ask your librarian.
Librarians are a store of valuable information—not all
having to do with books.

Learn to be alone, and enjoy it. Some days are so filled with
people and things that we don't have time to be alone. Or
we use people to protect us from loneliness. We also use
things—the television, the stereo, refrigerator, telephone,
or whatever keeps us from ourselves. People today are
suffering from a noisy heart, says Wayne Oates, a
professor at the University of Louisville Medical Center.
"If you are afraid of the loneliness and shrink back from
the adventure of searching for privacy because of it, you
will drop back into the drabness of the four great noises of
the human heart—fatigue, loss of perspective, poor
judgment, and confusion. . . ."[9]

We all need some time to ourselves, and this inevitably

means coping with our loneliness, even if we have to say no to a well-meaning friend. "In our world," writes Henri Nouwen, a modern contemplative and spiritual guide to thousands throughout the world, "we are constantly pulled away from our innermost self and encouraged to look for answers instead of listening to the questions. A lonely person has no inner time nor inner rest to wait and listen. He wants answers and wants them here and now. But in solitude we can pay attention to our inner self."[10]

Even a busy person can punctuate a tight schedule of appointments and activities with moments of solitude. It's taking time out for spiritual, mental, and physical recharging while still in the heat of the battle. It can be as simple as a brisk or leisurely walk during the lunch hour, a jog before or after work, even a little free-floating, noncreative "wool gathering" at a desk, a work bench, or while mopping the floor.

Earlier I quoted from Andy Rooney, who figured out that if we live to be eighty we would have 29,220 days to live. In his essay he indicated that he would like to sleep only two hours so that he could have more time to do what he wanted—like sitting and staring. This is not wasting time, he says. "We all need to do more of that and you can't speed up staring, and I wouldn't want to if I could."

I find the solitude I need when I'm mowing my grass or plunking at the typewriter in my room at one corner of our house. I can shut the door and sit in the middle of my "nest." Books, papers, and trash encircle me on the floor until a book or article has been mailed to the publisher. That's my corner and I can do what I want with it. That sacred place in my house has a history and memories. When I'm tense and pressured, I look forward to going there. It's not a place on the seashore or a cabin in the woods, *but it's my very own place.*

We all need that kind of place for solitude. The *Chicago*

Tribune Sunday Magazine recently carried a cover story about convicted robber Edward "Bear" Thomas, who lives in a tiny cell with a roommate at Illinois' Stateville Correctional Center. In the midst of tough and violent inmates, he works fifteen hours a day; and when he's feeling pressured, he retreats to a laundry room and tapes a sign on the door:

> If It's Not Police Business,
> Leave Me Be. It's Your Health.
> Don't Be No Fool. LEAVE ME ALONE.
>
> —Bear[11]

We cope with loneliness, not by always being with people, but by choosing sometimes to be alone. Each of us needs his or her own "laundry room" or "nest" away from the mindless din of our noisy world.

Cultivate friendship, but don't expect friends to protect you from loneliness. Have you ever caught yourself calling up a friend because you wanted to escape from something? A bad day? An angry encounter at work? A boring afternoon? It's legitimate to do that with friends. They can be present to us and we to them in moments of stress when it's important to talk, cry, or just be together. But we can also abuse our friends by demanding that they protect us from loneliness. We choke our solitude and inner space with what Anne Morrow Lindbergh calls "continuous music, chatter, and companionship to which we do not even listen."[12] We ask the impossible of them—to entertain us, to divert us.

Be aware of how you use friends, and then be honest with yourself and with them if you need them to help in a particularly difficult time. In confronting loneliness, it may not be as important to be with a friend as to know that a friend is near—the assurance that help is readily available if needed. It's knowing that in our loneliness there is another person who's thinking of us, but not interfering with the healing.

To enrich this most basic of human emotions, not to take it away—that's our task. But enrichment comes with experiencing and enduring, confronting and overcoming, being down and then rising to new strength. "We must re-learn to be alone," writes Lindbergh. In a society that decries loneliness as a kind of character fault and offers all kinds of palliatives to relieve it, we need to relearn how to face and live through loneliness. For most of us that means learning how to be alone with ourselves and live with the emptiness.

Let yourself be lonely sometimes. If loneliness is so much a part of living, why must we try to obliterate it entirely from our lives? Can we not learn from it?

Whenever I visit my home town in Ohio, I rarely miss visiting the graves of my parents. They are buried on the top of a knoll in a beautiful wooded and landscaped cemetery. Nearby are the graves of their friends and relatives. I go to remember, and to touch my own heritage. I experience loneliness. Kneeling, I touch and smell the grass and mostly sit and think. When I leave, I'm different, ready to get back to family and friends.

Do I want to be so insulated from love, from memory, from the world, and from myself that I never feel hurt? Do I want to be so out of touch with life's little pleasures that I never mourn my own death? Do I want to be so "together," so "adjusted" that I never know the satisfaction of being "at one" again with my world? Most of my growing in life has resulted from coming apart and getting back together again.

Nevertheless, voices all around us urge us to despise our bad days, to think something's wrong with us, to find clever ways of getting around them. Too many voices advise us to give in, give up, or duck around our bad days.

Resist obvious, unsatisfying, easy solutions!

Part Two
When Bad Days Get You Down

A bad day is any time you feel alienated from your environment, from other people, or from yourself. A bad day is feeling upset, off center, or out of sync, and not knowing exactly why. A bad day is starting out what appears to be a good day and suddenly the "tilt" sign lights up, warning you that the game is all over—at least for that day.

In the last section, we looked at common everyday causes of bad days—frustration, resentment, various kinds of threats, and loneliness, and I suggested specific ways of dealing with them—positive steps for living the bad days.

But because we are imperfect people, we can't always have perfect control of our world. Wherever one life intersects with another, someone is sure to disappoint or be disappointed, to criticize or be scolded, to get angry, to make a mistake, to pressure, or to infringe on the freedom of another.

Not only do we *not* have perfect control over other people and events, but each of us reacts differently to life's stresses. Some days we are better able to handle crises than other days; as energy levels change, one day might be better than another.

Occasionally bad days will get you down, no matter how strong you think you are. When that happens—when you feel vulnerable—you may take the easy way out. In this section we look at some of the ways we cope with bad days when we don't feel like facing them. We'll look at the telltale signs of giving in to the bad days, how we use convenient excuses to avoid taking responsibility, and favorite crutches for avoiding or evading life's rough spots.

See if you can identify your favorite tactic for avoiding the bad days.

5

Giving In to Bad Days

Do you know when you are going to have a bad day? I do. It starts out like this. Exhausted and off to bed, I try to force sleep, but hear each hour strike on the old mantel clock inherited from my grandfather twenty years ago. It's been tolling the wee hours of the night ever since Eli Terry and his son began making clocks in the late 1700s. It strikes two, three, and four o'clock. Restless, I know there's a full day ahead. Finally I doze off just as dawn breaks through the darkness. As the morning light comes into focus, yesterday's troubles, so neatly laid aside, begin to flood into the gray haze of consciousness. Legs heavy and tense, I draw them up close like an unborn baby taking warmth from its mother's womb. I shudder, throw back the blanket, and brave the few steps to the bathroom. "Maybe a good hot (or cold) shower will jolt me out of this mood," I think. But instead I become merely a washed, wide-awake bundle of nerves.

It's the beginning of another new day—a bad day—and I wonder how I will ever get through it. If only I could crumple it up and toss it aside like a shred of paper from the typewriter. Unfortunately, I can't deal with days that way. The new day stands there in the wings, twenty-four hours of it, beckoning me to enter center stage and play out the drama.

Maybe we decide the day is too painful, too demanding, too threatening. We look for an easier way; we call in sick and go back to bed. But what's been accomplished? We've ducked out on a bad day, but at what cost? What will we do when another bad day comes along, as it surely will? Because it was easy to avoid once, will avoidance be our style in the future?

Giving in to bad days—denying them, discounting them, making fun of them, or ducking out on them—creates other bad days. For instance, if something at work makes you angry and you avoid facing it, your frustration and resentment can create extra bad days. Energy goes into coping with this new circumstance, and not into dealing with the original problem.

Giving in to a problem, a circumstance, or a situation because it may cause you to have a bad day means that, instead of facing it, you let it tyrannize you. You let your fears and your anxieties keep you from confronting it. You let resentments and frustrations bully you into giving in or even giving up.

Giving in is the same as giving up. It's letting yourself be a victim and admitting that you have no power. It's living like an emotional pauper, picking up from the gutter what remnants of self-esteem you can garner from the trash that others have discarded.

Giving in is the first of three mechanisms we use to hang on to life rather than courageously live the bad days. If you are wondering whether you are merely surviving from day to day or living each day fully, examine yourself for these telltale signs of giving in.

Obsessive Fretting

One of the most tragic and isolated people I knew spent all her days fretting about how badly life had treated her. A bright career woman who once had a responsible government position, she had become bitter because of a series of events that resulted in her dismissal. To cut expenses and to conserve a meager income, she moved into the basement of her house and rented out the upstairs. There she lived in chilly isolation with her cat, brooding on ways to get even. Every waking minute she stewed in her own misery, calling anyone who would listen to her story. She bemoaned her helplessness, accused family and friends of conspiring to injure her, and blamed the community for being heartless and cruel.

She would call me and talk nonstop for an hour or more. If I tried to limit her, she would say, "You're just like all the rest—no time to listen to someone who needs help."

She pleaded for friendship, but seemed only to want an audience. I tried to connect her with potential friends (people who were untiringly patient and caring) but she soon sucked them dry by her endless wailing. Not once in all my visits as a minister did she try to discover who I was as a person. She had long ago given in to her bad days, retiring from friends and cultivating her misery.

Out of the pages of the Bible comes a classic account of obsessive fretting as Job, himself, reveals:

> Is not man's life on earth nothing more than pressed
> service,
> his time no better than hired drudgery?
> Like the slave, sighing for the shade,
> or the workman with no thought but his wages,
> months of delusion I have assigned to me,
> nothing for my own but nights of grief.
> Lying in bed I wonder, "When will it be day?"

Risen I think, "How slowly evening comes!"
Restlessly I fret till twilight falls. (7:1–4)

These two examples vividly illustrate obsessive fretting—certainly justified if you keep score on life, weighing justice against injustice, hurt against health. But I've known people who have suffered greatly, yet have handled it differently. They reel temporarily under the blows, but bounce back with greater courage than before.

Most of the obsessive fretters I know seem to have a self-indulgent, negative attitude toward everything, not because they have suffered and are trying to live with the pain, but because that's how they handle everything. If they feel frustrated, resentful, fearful, or lonely, instead of trying to solve a bad-day problem, obsessive fretters will just complain about it. Their attitude and complaint infects all who have to live or work with them. They never hear that portion of the weather report that says, "Tomorrow there is a fifty percent chance of sunshine." Instead, they notice only that there is a fifty percent chance of rain.

Obsessive fretting is the opposite of what one author calls "creative brooding." Obsessive fretting is circular thinking that goes nowhere. It is thinking that is stunted by its own narrow vision. Creative brooding, on the other hand, is the mind set free. It is thinking that knows no limits.

If you find yourself wearily telling friends how rottenly the world is treating you, rather than about specific problems you are facing, you are probably giving in to your bad days, letting them get you down.

By itself, obsessive complaining solves nothing. It bores our friends and sets us up for failure. We tend to fall in love with the sound of our own voice and the cadence of the story, until we have lost sight of the original problem and delight only in the suffering.

Making Light of Situations

Another telltale sign that we are giving in to bad days is when we make light of a situation instead of seeing the funniness of it. To make light of a bad day is to duck out on it, not take it seriously, avoid dealing with the problems it presents. It is hurting and pretending not to. It is a form of denial. On the other hand, to see the funniness of a thing is to take it seriously while picking at its absurdities.

Some days are so bad that all we can do is sit back and laugh through our tears—there's absolutely nothing we or anyone else can do to avoid them. They are there because we happen to be there. They are so exasperating that we can only hoist the white flag and say that we surrender.

Here's an example of what I mean. Not long ago I had a speaking engagement in Tuscaloosa, Alabama, a normally uneventful trip by plane. It was a warm, sunny day, perfect for flying. I had planned my trip so I would arrive about three hours before my seminar. The plane from Madison to Chicago's O'Hare airport was on time. But from O'Hare on, I experienced nothing but disaster. As the DC-9 jet pulled out of the flight gate, it suddenly turned around and went back. The doors opened and workers in overalls began to peer into banks of tubes, wires, and dials located behind the cockpit. The flight attendant assured us that it was a minor problem, soon to be repaired. But when she began to serve free cocktails, I worried. Since I had less than an hour at Memphis to make my next connection, I asked, How minor? and, How long? Forcing a smile, she said it would take about an hour. Then she revised it to an hour and a half. To miss that connection meant that a roomful of people at the University of Alabama would be meeting without me.

We arrived at Memphis predictably late and, as expected, I missed my scheduled connection. I walked what seemed like three miles to the ticket counter to learn that I could catch the last plane of the day to Tuscaloosa if I hurried back to the flight ramp to take a plane to Atlanta. With all my earthly possessions, I ran what seemed like three miles back to the ramp, only to learn that the Atlanta flight also would be thirty minutes late—the same airline that was delayed out of Chicago. As I boarded, I knew that making the connection in Atlanta would be close, but hope prevailed. Settling back in my seat with safety belt buckled, I heard the captain's voice on the intercom: "Ladies and gentlemen, I apologize for our delay, but we are 2000 pounds light on fuel, and a truck is on its way." At this moment, all hope of arriving the same day seemed dashed. I didn't know whether to scream in despair or commandeer the plane and fly there myself. Since I was too timid to scream and didn't know anything about flying airplanes, I decided that the day was so bad and so absurd, I'd try to salvage as much of it as I could. If I got there, fine, and if I couldn't, well. . . .

A delay by the connecting flight in Atlanta, another one of many, saved the day; and I arrived only thirty minutes late, eating a carryout dinner en route to the meeting. I can laugh about it now!

Consider this example of a common childhood situation—not too unfamiliar to adults, either—reported from a thirteenth-century Oriental manuscript:

> Ikkyu, the Zen master, was very clever even as a boy. His teacher had a precious teacup, a rare antique. Ikkyu happened to break this cup and was greatly perplexed. Hearing the footsteps of his teacher, he held the pieces of the cup behind him. When the master appeared, Ikkyu asked: "Why do people have to die?"
> "This is natural," explained the older man. "Everything has to die and has just so long to live."

Ikkyu, producing the shattered cup, added: "It was time for your cup to die."[1]

This story illustrates that, no matter how hard we try, plans can go awry with trouble piling up on trouble. A situation can become so crazy, for reasons totally outside our control, that our only sane response is to cry—or laugh—or both. To lose a sense of the ridiculous and the comic absurdity in our lives can mean that we are taking ourselves too seriously. To lose our sense of the ridiculous in the face of sorrow, frustration, or the totally topsy-turvy, can invite giving in and giving up to our bad days.

Letting Bad Days Win

The third telltale sign is what we today call "the bottom line." If we behave as if the bad days are winning, then we have given in.

Here's what I mean by letting the bad days win. From the outside, the world's tumbling in. Or that's how it seems. Because of frustration, resentment, fear, or loneliness, it appears we have lost control, that events are pushing and pulling us in directions we don't want to go. To return to the pinball analogy, we put in our coin, ready to play, only to have the tilt sign light up. Anyone looking on will surely agree that we've been defeated.

But the bad days don't have to win. No matter how bad things seem outside, what's important is how we handle them inside. Call it spirit, morale, courage—real winning or losing is inside ourselves.

Life as a prisoner of war at the Kwai River in World War II—the theme of many books and films—illustrates the tension between external and internal survival. Ernest Gordon, now chaplain emeritus of Princeton University, reports how some prisoners, considered too sick to live and dragged to makeshift morgues, cared for one another. They took the rags from their own bodies, washed them, and bound the wounds of those who were worse off. *Living* began to replace *survival* as the prisoners looked beyond their own predicament to the higher needs of the bowed, but unbroken, human spirits. Wounded and tired bodies did not hurt any less. But as they looked beyond their despair, they caught a vision, sighted a goal, and dreamed a dream to lift them from the muck and rancidity of their existence.[2] The bad days pounded hard but could not win.

Here is another example of how one man facing death kept the bad days from winning. For nearly thirty years, I have kept a letter from a cousin who, from the age of six, had to endure the crippling effects of muscular dystrophy. As a child, I remember visiting him as he lay in bed or sat propped up in a wheelchair. The sun always shone around Don. His world view was much larger than the small room that was his home. He rarely talked about himself so that he could be with the friends and visitors who came to see him. The sun never set on his vigorous spirit.

Here's part of that letter, written on October 4, 1953:

> My life is quite restricted now, of course—physically that is. But I put my mental faculties to use on many varied fields and still enjoy life to the fullest extent possible.
>
> The past few months, since last spring, my general health has declined rapidly, however. Due to a liver congestion and resultant effects on heart, lungs, digestion, etc. So logically viewed it seems to me the sands of time are running out, as I don't believe there's much chance of improvement and I can't maintain the "status quo" indefinitely. But there's little use to speculate on the future. I always liked those lines from the Rubaiyat by Omar Khayaam where he wrote—"Come, let us make the most

of what we yet may spend, before we too into the dust descend—dust to dust and under dust to lie—sans wine, sans song, sans singer and sans end."

Well, Jim, enough of this philosophizing and chit-chatter. Am enclosing a small snapshot taken last Christmas of myself. But due to the liver I haven't been up in the wheelchair ever since last March thereabout. Horizontal or vertical tho', I'm still the same guy—a few pounds lighter now also—and always a "big stiff"—a slang expression, but descriptive in terms of arthritic effects.

My best regards to you and if possible, drop me a few lines. As always, your cousin, Don.

This brave young man died a few months later at age thirty-three. He had organized his days, not around death, but around living. Invalid and dying, he had achieved a health of spirit that out-lived his physical decline. He refused to give in to his bad days.

Look at Don's letter again. Instead of complaint (obsessive fretting) there's a vision beyond his own infirmity; instead of avoidance (making light of the situation), he looks at its absurdity; and instead of giving in (letting the bad days win), he declares his own victory over disease and death.

I was too young to really know or appreciate my cousin Don Acton. But his neatly scripted letter is one of my most precious treasures; tangible encouragement on the bad days.

6

Grabbing Convenient Excuses

Bad days are as normal as the movement of the tide, or the rising and setting of the sun. There are bad days because we happen to be at the wrong place at the wrong time. Bad days come because of circumstances over which we have no control, through no fault of our own.

Also we have bad days because of our own stupidities: because we did not face a frustration, work through a resentment, cope well with threat, face up to loneliness, or handle a thousand-and-one other causes.

Some people give in to bad days—they let the bad days win. Others look for the convenient excuse because it's easier than trying to work on the problem. Instead of considering *how* to resolve a frustration, work on a resentment, or manage threat or loneliness, they look instead at the *why*. Somehow, if we can come up with a plausible excuse, then we won't have to take responsibility for living through the bad days. We can play the role of victim and get off the hook. Inventing an excuse gives the illusion that we have found an answer when we've only pinned the responsibility on something or someone other than ourselves.

You know that the bad days are getting you down when

you begin to look for excuses instead of tackling the problem. Here are three common excuses: (a) blaming things that break down or go wrong, (b) blaming people who make stupid mistakes, and, when you are desperate, (c) blaming a deity who's just "stepped out."

Blaming Things That Break Down or Go Wrong

Again I come back to my favorite essayist of the obvious, Andy Rooney, who can draw out three hundred words or so on the hassles of taking a shower. (By the way, technology has increased the possibility of bad days as we become more and more dependent upon things that break down or go wrong.) Rooney once did a piece on soap. Many of us are constantly removing it from the shower floor or picking it out of the drain. Says Rooney:

> It's more like a thin cookie. It's not only too small, it's too sharp around the edges. No one wants sharp soap. The fact is, a cake of soap is only at its best for two or three days, while you can still feel the letters on it. I'd like to be rich enough to throw soap away after the letters have worn off.[1]

Another piece he did on plumbing fixtures brought back memories of a near-ruined day when I tried to install a do-it-yourself bathroom sink. The directions imply that everyone ought to understand what goes where, but that usually leaves out the weekend plumber grappling with that gaping void on the bathroom wall where there's supposed to be a sink. You drive back and forth between house and hardware store on a Saturday afternoon trying to explain your problem to the young clerk who was just hired yesterday. He doesn't know any more than you do, but tries to fake it. You take a piece of pipe home, and it almost works, except it's just a quarter inch too short. It neither stretches nor bends into position. Fifteen minutes from closing time, you're in the middle of a project that "a child can do." Sunday's just around the corner and you face a weekend without water. That's frustration! That's a certain bad day.

You swear at the sink, the pipe, and the hardware store, the writer of the directions, and even the plastic package that promises the five-easy-steps. All are guilty. All provide convenient, if not plausible excuses for this awful day.

The fact that you failed to heed one important instruction in the booklet is immaterial: "Don't start until you have read all the directions first." Someone else is at fault.

Look at another example, common to all who own and maintain automobiles. When something goes wrong, we look to the most convenient excuse first—the thing that broke down. Things are the most frustrating of all because they can't be talked to. They don't fight back. They are just there—all broken and not working. Like the water pump on your car. Its failure is usually sudden and total, nearly always timed to coincide with your vacation—not before you leave home, but after.

Things frustrate us because we are so dependent upon them. They provide ready and convenient excuses for our bad days. So do people who make stupid mistakes.

Blaming People Who Make Stupid Mistakes

Frustration is finding yourself stranded along the freeway with the red warning light inside your car flashing and the coolant running from your radiator. You just had the car checked out before this vacation: "If that mechanic had only done his job properly, this would never have happened! I'll give him a piece of my mind."

Resentment and threats to our self-esteem prompt us to blame others for the bad days that overtake us. "I wouldn't feel this way if Jack hadn't. . . ." "This day started out pretty well, until Martha. . . ." "If I go to that meeting tonight, Bill will ruin my whole week. . . ." "If I didn't have to pick up after the whole family all the time, I could go to a night class without being exhausted and hassled."

"All blame is a waste of time," says psychologist Wayne Dwyer. "No matter how much fault you find with another, and regardless of how much you blame him, it will not change you. The only thing blame does is keep the focus off you when you are looking for external reasons to explain your unhappiness or frustration."[2]

It is inevitable that people we live with, work with, and are friends with, can intentionally or unintentionally cause us grief. But also remember that we may also cause others pain because of something we've said or done. The closer people are to each other emotionally, the more volatile the relationship and susceptible to misunderstandings, hurt feelings, and frustration.

It is a thin line indeed between blaming people for making *stupid mistakes* and blaming *stupid people* for mistakes. When we feel frustrated or resentful—the foundations of many bad days—we don't draw the line too clearly, especially when we're angry. The problem with looking to others for excuses is that we often combine blaming with punishment. We inflict hurt upon the object of our blame, which bruises relationships, and clearly moves away from problem solving. *Stupid behavior* easily becomes confused with *stupid people*. The original problem—the faulty water pump—may get mended in the midst of angry blaming. But at what cost to ourselves? To the others?

When the previous excuses fail—blaming things that go wrong or blaming others for stupid mistakes—the last resort is blaming God for taking a lunch break just when we need him.

Blaming a Deity Who's Just Stepped Out

Blaming God for bad days is the perfect excuse when all others fail. It is also the ultimate cry of surrender when we let bad days get us down. It is the lament of a character from one of Peter DeVries' novels: "Oh, God, is this what I deserve?" The assumption is that God is somehow responsible for our suffering—the excuse of last resort.

The problem of suffering and God's role in it has plagued theologians for centuries. In the Old Testament, Job is clearly caught in the middle of a dilemma. He affirms his faith in God (Yahweh):

> Naked I came from my mother's womb,
> naked I shall return.
> Yahweh gave, Yahweh has taken back.
> Blessed be the name of Yahweh.   (1:21)

But the other side of Job's dilemma is also there. Why did God step out (to lunch, for a breath of fresh air, or whatever) just at that moment in his life when Job really needed him?

> Why give light to a man of grief?
> Why give life to those bitter of heart. . .
> Why make this gift of light to a man who does not see his
>   way,
> whom God balks on every side?   (3:20–23)

Jesus rejected the idea that suffering of any kind was tied either to a person's wrongdoing or to God's direct intervention in a person's life. In fact, whenever Jesus saw pain, he tried to relieve it. God does not say, "Jim, today

I'm going to make you fall and break a leg because you have lied," or "because you need to learn something about carelessness." I may indeed fall and break a leg, but I do it because I have made an unwise choice to climb to the top of a rickety ladder. Or it could be that I did not see the ice patch covered with snow.

Still, the great and haunting question of the centuries is, "If God is God, why does he allow suffering?" Leslie D. Weatherhead, a London preacher and pioneer in pastoral psychology, is helpful at this point:

> I want to point out the essential difference between believing that God sends specific disease, *intending* the individual to suffer anguish as punishment for something done, and believing that God has put us into a universe where dangerous factors operate which, through our ignorance, folly or sin, may bring suffering to us. It is one thing to take a man by main force and thrust him between the rollers of some huge machine in an engineering shop. It is another thing to give him a job in the engineering shop where there is dangerous machinery in which he may get cut up and mangled if he does not know how to work the machinery, if he is careless or foolish, or if a fellow-workman pushes him—through folly or sin—against unguarded wheels . . . .
>
> . . . God does not will suffering, but . . . He cannot achieve His own higher purposes if He made a universe from which all possibility of suffering was excluded. He is therefore responsible that there is such a thing as suffering. Yet no one could say of any particular bit of suffering, 'This is the will of God.'[3]

For those of us who believe in God—whether Jew, Muslim, or Christian—who affirm that God creates and continues to be at work in the universe, it does at times seem that he has just stepped out. Bad days have a way of isolating us like that, making us feel alone and out-of-touch, even with God. Blaming God then becomes the next logical step in the alienation. It's easy to blame a spouse, a friend, or even God when we feel isolated from the relationship. Blaming is how we get even. It's poking for attention: "Look, here I am. Pay attention to me."

But why does God appear to be always "out" when we need him? Do you know what I mean? We face some particularly sticky situation. We try to pray. But we don't sense anything happening like stars flashing, or a voice inside, or a voice anywhere. Praying, we don't know if anybody's listening. Maybe God has stepped out to take care of a Middle East war or some big tragedy in Tibet.

It's easy to find an excuse for bad days in a God who's too busy.

Nevertheless, maybe the problem is not that God is too busy, but that the bad days have gotten us down. And we substitute excuses for the sweat of working through the answers.

7

Leaning on Crutches

Another way we try to survive the bad days is by leaning on crutches. Crutches come in many varieties and sizes.

Chemicals

The ease with which Americans turn to alcohol, drugs, and prescription medications to calm them down and pep them up is alarming. The alcohol and drug toll in deaths, wasted lives, and anesthetized existence is beyond description. Nearly half the people in our country drink, and more than nine million are alcohol abusers. Loss of productivity and damage to life and property are conservatively estimated at $15 billion annually.

Drug abuse reaches into the youngest populations. Where once a furtive cigarette was thought to be wicked, now tobacco is only the beginning. The hard stuff—alcohol, cocaine, amphetamines, barbiturates, heroin—are commonplace. One ten-year-old boy commented recently on television that he had kicked the drug habit. He reported proudly that, confronting a minor problem, he had decided not to "turn on."

When something's wrong, the American way is to fix it with a shot of whiskey, a pep pill, or an aspirin. According to Donald Ardell, editor of the *American Journal of Health Planning,* people in this country average more than 225 aspirin tablets per person annually, consuming an untold amount as a nation. When aspirin doesn't work, then we turn to Valium and Librium, the two anxiety-reducing staples of our national medication diet, estimated to end up on prescriptions from 75 percent of all doctor visits. Ardell continues:

> Spend an hour before the tube and you will be assaulted by the pharmaceutical industry with offers of pills or other nostrums for improved sleep, excretion, energy, youthfulness, smell, and naturally, overall health. Mood elevators, amphetamines, tranquilizers, narcotic pain pills, and antihistamines seem more American than apple pie, which is bad enough![1]

As a young pastor comforting survivors of auto accidents or families of sudden heart attack victims, I noticed that the first help some friends offered at such times was a sedative. All it did, as far as I could tell, was to defer the symptoms of shock. Shocks as deep and as soul-wrenching as the death of a loved one need a clear head for grief's difficult, but healing, journey. While sedatives and other chemical crutches often blunt the normal first-impact symptoms, with continued use they also dull the shine on good days.

Limited Warranties

Besides alcohol, drugs, and prescription medications, another crutch for handling the bad days is to take out a limited warranty insurance policy on life—that is, to calculate the risks and limit your vulnerability to potential hurt by avoiding the risks altogether. If you don't go down the ski hill, you won't fall and break a leg. If you don't tell a friend that you love him or her, you won't be rejected. If you bottle up angry feelings, then a co-worker can't strike back.

We reason that if we construct a cocoon of safety around ourselves by limiting our liability to frustration, resentment, threat, and loneliness—common causes of bad days—then surely we will be happy. This is what Nena and George O'Neill in *Shifting Gears* call "the guarantee hang-up." According to the O'Neills, this myth says that if we think the right thoughts, do the right things, and reduce risks, everything will turn out all right. Troubles and bad days will disappear.

But such thinking is sheer manipulation, says Everett Shostrom, a student of contemporary American behavior.

> The manipulator is legion. He is all of us, consciously, subconsciously, or unconsciously employing all the phoney tricks we absorb between the cradle and grave to conceal the actual vital nature of ourselves and, in the process, reducing ourselves and our fellow man into things to be controlled.[2]

Obviously, there are certain predictable and insurable risks against which we have to protect ourselves, like financial disaster due to the catastrophic losses of fire, death, and illness. It's just good life planning to insure against potential destruction of life and property. But when we try to insure ourselves against bad days, we so isolate ourselves that we miss the most important parts of life—loving, hurting, healing, forgiving, engaging, facing problems, and overcoming them.

To organize our lives to shun anything bad means we must go through frequent and unusual physical and mental contortions to reduce our risks—to protect our "limited warranty" lives. We invariably cut ourselves off from others in this kind of self-imposed quarantine.

I thought about this a few days ago when I saw a cover story in the Baton Rouge *Sunday Advocate* magazine on J. D. Salinger, the author and creator of Holden Caulfield in *Catcher in the Rye*. Betty Eppes, a staff journalist, went to Vermont to find out why one of America's most popular and controversial authors vanished, or at least adopted a limited warranty strategy for living. Here's what she reported:

The article said that Salinger, sixty-two, wants to be left alone. He refuses autographs and speaks to few people on his visits to neighboring Windsor. An author who dared to explore adolescent alienation through the adventures of Holden Caulfield, Salinger pleads with his interviewer, "Why can't I be left alone?" The motivation behind those words was not clear to journalist Eppes.

> Watching his tall agile figure disappear into the shadows, questions floated up in my mind. If J. D. Salinger is sincere in his desire for the hermit's life, why come nine miles to talk with an absolute stranger? Could it be that he wants to be remembered and read, but isn't willing to pay the price for remembrance? Rethinking our encounter, I must turn Salinger's stock question back on him—J. D., why did you come?[3]

Why does this famous author remain aloof? For solitude? Because he's afraid of people? To be spared pain or even love? To preserve a limited warranty on his remaining years? We can only guess and wonder.

Collecting Approval Points

We know the bad days are getting to us when we find ourselves giving in to them, when we look for convenient excuses, or when we depend upon crutches to avoid or survive them. The difficulty with crutches is that they can become habit-forming, though we intend them to be only temporary. An occasional drink or pill to get through the day can easily become a frequent drink or two pills instead of one. The decision to take a limited warranty approach to risks during a particularly rough period can readily become a permanent, continuing mode of living.

When bad days get us down, we sometimes collect what I call "approval points"; the words, glances, and smiles that tell us we are okay. Because we depend upon the respect of others, we collect any kind of tangible affirmation that will tell us we are okay when bad days come along. That's not a bad thing to do, because we all need to be loved and to know we're okay, but being obsessive about it and trying to get them at any cost can be harmful.

There are at least two hazards in collecting approval points at any cost. One is the price we pay within ourselves when we put our own feelings and wants on "hold." We pay the price in frustration, anger, and resentment, creating the very same bad days we are trying to avoid in the first place. Not only that, but we set ourselves up for a no-win situation. By trying to build up self-worth by getting the approval of people, we can lose it. Inside, we know we have "sold out" in order to please. For a time, we succeed. But within ourselves, we feel hollow.

A second hazard in collecting approval points is that no matter how much we turn ourselves inside-out to please, we always risk falling short of expectation—not doing enough. Psychologist Dwyer cautions:

> Take a look at the way the world works. To put it succinctly, you can never please everybody. In fact, if you please fifty percent of the people, you are doing quite well.

This is no secret. You know that at least half of the people in your world are going to disagree with half the things you say. If this is accurate (and you need only look at landslide elections to see that forty-four percent of the population still voted against the winner), then you will always have about a 50–50 chance of getting disapproval whenever you express an opinion.[4]

But in the scurrying for respect and approval, Dwyer's counsel falls aside. Many of us still carry with us the faint hope that if we work hard to please, and if we strive for perfection, we will stave off disapproval.

Just the opposite is true. The more you meet the expectations of others—even when you don't feel like it, because you need their approval—the more people expect of you. With increased expectations, the possibilities for failure also increase, bringing on (you guessed it) more bad days.

Take comfort in Merl Shain's advice, a Toronto writer and television commentator. She says:

> It is very difficult to accept the fact that there are no guarantees in life, no guarantees that life will progress as it should or that the people you care about will love you back, or even that they will treat you right. But trust in life does not mean trusting that life will always be good or that it will be free of grief and pain. It means trusting that somewhere inside yourself you can find the strength to go forth and meet what comes and, even if you meet betrayal and disappointment along the way, go forth again the very next day.[5]

In this section I've argued that bad days are inevitable when we meet frustration, harbor resentment, face threats, and cope with loneliness. But when these stresses get us down, we find evasive or destructive ways of handling them such as giving in, looking for excuses, or hanging onto crutches. Instead of taking the hard road that often leads to growth and self-knowledge, we settle for the easy path. Instead of living the bad days, we merely survive them, and live only partial lives.

Living the bad days is like driving down an ice-coated highway and going into a skid. Fight the wheel and you'll likely spin out. But slide with the skid, turn into it, and you'll probably come out of it scared and shaken, but safe, and perhaps wiser about how to drive on hazardous roads.

Part Three
Living the Bad Days

Living the bad days is more than just hanging onto life by a cobweb. Living the bad days is facing problems at their worst—frustration, resentment, threats, and loneliness—accepting difficulty as a normal part of day-to-day living.

Bad days afflict the educated and the uneducated, the rich and the poor, those that "have it together" and people "coming apart." To be alive is to see both good and bad days.

Bad days teach us, help us grow, prepare us for tomorrow. They give as much to life as they take from it. And we can decide how to spend the bad days. We can give in to them, drink our way through them, medicate against them, pretend they don't exist, or find convenient excuses.

Or we can live them!

Part Three encourages you to step up to your next bad day as you might venture to cross an unknown river, without a bridge, to get to the other side. Scared, you jump in, feeling the sting of the cold water. You take a risk without guarantees. You learn to trust yourself (and God), to solve difficult problems, to laugh at the ridiculous, or if nothing else works, to muddle through in the certainty that everything in life has an ultimate meaning.

8

What Bad Days Teach Us

Christina, a pretty, soft-spoken, and unhappy legal secretary, came to see me the other day "just to talk with someone." Apologizing for taking my time, she got to the point of her visit quickly: "I feel trapped! All my life I have tried to please others. Now I want to do something for myself, but I don't know if I can."

Embarrassed, she added, "I live at home. Would you believe that I am nearly thirty-five years old and still live at home with my parents? What must you think of me?" She talked about her parents and her reluctance to take even a brief holiday from them.

"I've traded my freedom for security," she said, "And I don't know if I can change. I feel so miserable."

"Why haven't you moved into an apartment of your own?" I asked.

"I'm afraid," Christina answered. "Afraid of being alone, of hurting my parents, of not wanting to disappoint them. The bad days are unbearable—the tension—wanting to change but terrified that I'll make a mistake. That's it, I'm afraid of failing."

There were tears in her large brown eyes as she asked, "What shall I do?" But she didn't wait for an answer. "You might not think so, but I'm really a very strong person."

"I'm sure you are," I replied, wondering if the hurt and this first step into my office would be enough to pull her through the months to come. We talked about her dreams for the future, the risks and the hazards. There would be no guarantees. She seemed anguished as she struggled with the cost of living free. Dare she risk the hurt and loneliness? Her words showed that she wanted to change direction in her life, but her slumped posture communicated despair.

Christina's situation is not unusual. For many of us, early choices, or even those as late as last year or last week, no longer work. We pay for those early choices with bad days. We have outgrown past decisions. We want our lives to be different, but are reluctant to pay the price. We look at the cost, the trade-offs, the compromises, and we hesitate. Do we have the courage to try a new direction? Though the status quo may make us sick, what if we change and it doesn't work out?

During the hour or so that Christina and I talked, she pondered the alternatives, worried about the consequences, and left, still feeling trapped.

Her dilemma illustrates the inner turmoil that many of us go through as we try to understand the bad days. We feel the frustration, the resentment, the threats to our security, and the loneliness. But what do they mean? Can any good possibly come out of them? Do they have meaning beyond their own unique misery? That's the key issue of this chapter as we reflect on how we can learn and grow from the bad days.

Bad Days Have Meaning

"What do we possess save faith that there is a God, a time of hereafter; that there may be a way that all events, all

96

things have meaning?" writes Wisconsin folklore author Robert Gard in *Innocence of Prairie*. Gard continues, "Every person's world may be a child's world to be used, appreciated, preserved and celebrated every moment."[1]

We often have to look beyond a worrisome day to understand what the day means. An illustration: You may ponder how to work out a conflict with the boss at work and consider alternative solutions. But the ultimate meaning of that conflict and your response to it may not be known until two days, a week, or a year later. Meaning has to do with how this event fits into your total life pattern, how it influences the rest of your life, as well as other conflicts you will experience.

Imagine for a moment that you could step out of yourself and look down on your life as if you were standing over a giant, partially completed jigsaw puzzle. Notice the lines, colors, patterns, and textures of the completed areas. Think of the pieces of the puzzle as specific life events, each with contrasting tones and moods. There's schooling, friendships, marriage or singleness, children, the first job, and the second. They make up the unique picture that is you.

But there are missing pieces. Events have happened, but you don't know how they fit into the puzzle. Or the events have not yet happened but will find their place in the puzzle at a later time. For example, a conflict with the boss may not make any sense at all until other pieces have fallen into place.

Whether an event has meaning depends upon how we approach the key questions: "Who am I? What am I doing? Why am I doing what I'm doing? Where am I going? What's my motivation? Do I want to be where I am? Would I be happier if I were someplace else or doing something else?" As you look at each piece of your life-puzzle, these are the questions that help shape the picture, that give it meaning.

Meanings have a way of jumping out at us by an unexpected series of events, surprising us and catching us off guard. We've made a mistake, avoided dealing with a problem, tried to short-cut our own best judgment, and come up with a bad day. Maybe a whole series of them. We didn't plan our life that way, and the bad day is unwelcome. Nevertheless, that single bad day or bunch of them may have meaning beyond anyone's immediate comprehension, as related in this story told by a friend.

While traveling in England some years ago, our brand new VW was hit in a British "turn-around"—our fault. Fortunately, no one was hurt, but the axle was broken and would cost nearly all our last month's travel money to repair. The collision insurance would have cost over $200 for the three months of our trip abroad, so we had decided to risk doing without it. During the two weeks our car was being fixed, we took a train to London, walked five miles to Longleat House, hitchhiked to Bath, and wrote home for loans from our parents. After spending all but our last two pounds on car repairs, we drove to Edinburgh, trusting the money from home would be there waiting for us. It didn't come for another week! We slept in a beach house one night, in the car another, and finally convinced a Scottish bed-and-breakfast innkeeper that we could pay when our money arrived. Every day we spent what seemed like endless hours waiting at American Express for the money that took what seemed like years to arrive. We were broke, stranded, and miserable.

The whole experience was a disaster and a mess . . . three weeks full of bad days . . . yet it gave us some of the most fondly remembered days of our lives. Without the car crash, we might never have experienced the kindly generosity, hospitality, and trust of the Scottish and English people. We would have missed traveling in a wonderful English train compartment, or walking miles through rolling country lanes lined with stone-walled pastures, seeing things we would never have seen by car. Seeking things to do for free, we visited obscure museums and spent the most beautiful day of our lives wandering through the glass houses, rock gardens, art gallery and lush rhododendrons of the Edinburgh botanical gardens—a day that inspired my present passion for rock gardening. We've forgotten how miserable we were sleeping with spiders in the damp beach house and waking up with cramped bones after a night in the VW—instead we keep the memories of beautiful days and the interests we found during those weeks that will keep us busy and happy throughout our lives.

As my friend told that story, she seemed to be in a time capsule, reliving what was now a precious memory—but at the time were bad days.

Don't Squander Your Inner Strength

Inner strength is feeling good about yourself. It's what gets you up in the morning and through the day. It's the energy and the motivation that you put into living. Without this inner strength, you feel tired, listless, as if you're merely stringing together the events, problems, and situations of your life with your presence. You feel little enthusiasm for anything.

Inner strength is different from the power that money and property bestow. Howard Hughes, one of the wealthiest people on earth, was also one of the most fragile. He was afraid to walk ten steps from his bed for fear of catching an unfriendly germ. He could buy anything he wanted except inner strength.

Every time we look into the mirror we see how we look

to others. But we see our inner image as well. People spend millions of dollars in the marketplace and on psychiatrists' couches trying to acquire self-worth and inner strength. We read books and magazines or look to family and friends to help us find it. We feel good when we have it and sick when we don't.

Most people take this inner strength for granted. They let hostility in a marriage, or an overbearing boss, or a thoughtless co-worker chip away at it. In Christina's case, her inner strength had eroded over the years because she allowed other people to tell her how to live. She had never declared her independence. She traded security for freedom—and the risks that go with freedom. Early in life she had learned to live inside protective barriers that family and friends willingly put around her. Now bad days had invaded her tight, secure, limited warranty world. Could her life change? Christina would have to discover that for herself.

Any day that questions the status quo, prods apathy, or stirs you to constructive action can give an unexpected meaning to your life. Sometimes the so-called detours are more exciting and meaningful than the well-traveled and too-familiar main highways.

Siddhartha, the aging mystic hero of Herman Hesse's novel of that name, spent a lifetime looking for the meaning of his bad days. Nearing the end of his life, he confided to his friend, Govinda:

> I learned through my body and soul that it was necessary for me to . . . experience nausea and the depths of despair in order to learn not to resist them, in order to learn to love the world, and no longer compare it with some kind of desired imaginary world, some imaginary vision of perfection, but to leave it as it is, to love it, and be glad to belong to it.[2]

The meaning of a bad day or situation is in how we feel

about it and in what it adds to or subtracts from our life. Does it increase our inner strength or take from it? Inner strength is the ability to get up in the morning, to face the day as it comes, and feel confident at the end of the day.

Yet meaning can come from the struggle, the fight to survive a bad day. Inner strength comes more often from facing a problem and overcoming it, or even failing, than it does from easy living. We learn from both successes and failures. It's not the failures that do us in, it's letting our inner strength slip away because we let others decide our future and even our present.

Inner strength comes from the way we put together past events, relationships, and experiences to meet today's events, relationships, and experiences. We may have just enough inner power to get by, or we may have more than we need—or less. It's like electricity. Just enough power lights our homes and takes care of ordinary needs. If we have a reserve, we can meet emergency needs. Or, like low voltage electricity that blows fuses under too much load, we sometimes shut down under too much stress, and feel upset, exhausted, and self-protecting.

While bad days do put an extra load on our inner strength, that doesn't mean we have to automatically "shut down." Difficult problems can either drain our power reserves, or add to them as we struggle to find answers. Sometimes it's not easy to know whether bad days add to or subtract from our inner strength. Bad days may mean that we're no longer in control of our life and it's time to make drastic changes. Or the bad days may call forth previously untapped inner resources to help us work through a difficult time.

Either way, they prod us to ask, "What am I learning from these bad days, this misery?" Coming up with a clearly defined answer to this question may not be as important as suffering through the process of discovery—feeling helpless, and daring to try something different.

Returning to Christina's situation, here are three suggestions that could turn her bad days into important new lessons.

Practice taking charge of today. Christina hadn't had much experience at doing this. She generally reacted to other people's decisions at great cost to her own sense of worth. Who's in charge of your "today?" Think back over the past month or so. Write down on a piece of paper the events you made happen. Note the friends you called up or invited out to lunch. Note the problems that you took initiative to solve. But also look at the times you merely reacted to events. How many times in the past month did you sit back and wait for someone else to call, to invite, or to apologize? Taking charge of today is a way of life for thousands of formerly chemically dependent people whose bad days have caused them to change their lives.

The recovering drug abuser or alcoholic, for example, cannot claim to be cured, or promise not to stumble tomorrow. All energy goes into facing "today." For the chemically dependent, it means getting through the day without taking a drink or pill.

To practice taking charge of today means that you meet each situation or problem as it comes and do something that involves taking charge rather than merely reacting. It could be as simple as deciding how you want to spend your day and doing just that. If you are a mother with small children at home, a decision to take the afternoon off may mean arranging for a babysitter.

People who merely react to life often complain about not having enough time to do what they want because they are so busy doing something else. Reactors are always waiting for opportunities. On the other hand, people who practice taking charge of their days make their own opportunities. They don't wait until they have free time. They *make* free time to do what they want. So you might start taking charge of today by deciding how to use your time more as you want to.

The key to practicing any skill, from learning how to sew, to flycasting for trout, to taking charge of today, is just *doing* it. Don't worry about coming up with the perfect plan, or solution, or answer. What's important is the effort. It is trying, failing, and starting all over again. It's learning from your successes as well as your mistakes.

Once you gain some experience and success at taking charge, you'll discover that you have more control over your life than you may have thought. At least, you'll be more discerning of situations you can and cannot influence directly. And that is a major lesson.

Accept change as normal. Nothing stays the same. By the time we have solved one problem, a new one takes its place. As we grow older, we change—hair turns from brown to gray, ideas once held sacred are discarded for new ones, and relationships grow closer or more distant. Change is inevitable. Inner strength comes from accepting the inevitable and using it to our advantage.

People who merely react instead of taking charge have a lot of trouble with change. It is just one more irritation to be endured, one more interruption in a neat and orderly world, one more proof that it's a dog-eat-dog world and you have to make sure you don't get "done in." A reactor looks at change defensively, as if stepping through a mine-field.

Accepting change involves welcoming and creating helpful change, and heading off harmful or exploitive change. Accepting change is becoming part of the good—changing with the change. On the other hand, some changes are not good—either private or public. Accepting change is not blind submission to anything that's different. It is creating conditions to make a zoning variance, for example, be responsive to the public interests. Should the neighborhood have high-density apartments? What will be the impact on the environment, on transportation, on schools? Accepting change is looking at what's happening around you, and becoming part of the movement. It is recognizing that with movement there can be growth. Inner growth comes when we participate in change, rather than only react to it.

Trust your own experience. We undercut our own inner strength and self-esteem when we undervalue our own experiences and rely solely upon the judgments of other people. In a society where there is an expert for everything, it's easier to hand over parts of our lives to experts than to fix things ourselves. We call the plumber to fix the faucet, the doctor to fix a cold, the lawyer to mediate a family dispute, the police to quiet a neighbor's dog, and the psychiatrist to talk to a grieving friend. No wonder we feel so helpless and powerless when we have to deal with run-of-the-mill situations ourselves—a neighbor angry about our wayward dog, frustration with a local hardware store manager, loneliness in the evening hours, or the fear that a job will collapse. There are no specialists to handle these feelings and situations for us the way a service representative can fix a broken furnace.

Inner strength is being able to act in a situation from our own experience and to trust that experience, even if the situation doesn't work out exactly as we want it. A take-charge or self-directed person trusts his or her experience, even without firm guarantees of success. A reactor, on the other hand, doesn't think his or her experience has much value.

Bad days and their demands add to our experience-bank, as well as test our power to deal with them. In other words, we learn from the bad days as we search for meanings, as we struggle for answers, and as we try to counter their harshness. It is this learning that builds our margin of power, giving us the courage and the resources to cope with whatever comes along.

9

Choosing Our Own Future

By the time we're conscious of how bad a day is, we are usually in the middle of it. It's like being sick; we don't think or worry about health until we're ill. Nevertheless, there's a whole future of bad days—those silent, wounding missiles of unhappiness—lurking somewhere in the future, because of us!

We often set up the good or bad days of tomorrow by the choices we make today. Think about yourself right at this very moment. Think of all the decisions made five, ten, fifteen years ago that helped shape today—a thoughtful decision, a careless decision, or a decision avoided. Our tomorrows are shaped by our todays; choices acted upon, avoided, or given over to someone else because we feel helpless and depressed.

Too often we mortgage tomorrow's joy because we make faulty decisions or we procrastinate for one reason or other. For instance, how many times have you been frustrated because of choices made or avoided one or two days earlier? Or resentful because you didn't handle a hurt or slight at the time it happened? How often have you said "yes" to some demand because you didn't want to feel guilty or hurt someone's feelings—and then regretted it later?

Every time you say no or yes to a request, demand, or invitation, you decide some part of your future. If you keep a calendar on the pantry door or an appointment book on your desk, look at it. It's a statement of how you will spend the hours and days of your future.

Whenever we're dealing with the future, it's difficult to predict with any accuracy how those tomorrows will turn out. Nor are there sure-fire systems for making error-free choices. Still, choosing and deciding cannot be left to whim or chance. In this chapter we look at how we make decisions, a process that follows logical and sequential stages no matter what expert is writing about it. I have adapted from the five stages of decision-making recently outlined by psychologists Daniel D. Wheeler and Irving L. Janis in one of the best popular discussions I've seen on this topic.

While no one can avoid risks, say the authors, "effective decision-making methods can help you assess the risks involved and can enable you to pick which risks you want to take."[1] Short of being a clairvoyant, able to avoid mistakes by reading the future, being able to pick our risks is indeed an acceptable alternative. Here are the five stages of responsible decision-making.

Stage 1. Accepting the Challenge

We have many bad days because our decisions don't clearly reflect what we *want* or how we really *feel* about something. Deciding to decide is the first (and basic) decision. Deciding to take an action (or not to act at all) is probably the most important decision. It's the "flywheel" decision. Though it takes a lot of push and effort to get going on a problem, once we've decided to overcome our hesitation and procrastination, we begin to create and draw on inner strength important in choosing our future. It's a lot like the electrical system on a car. Power from the battery makes the car run, but while it runs, power flows back to the battery with extra to spare.

In Christina's situation, her three-hundred-mile trip from Iowa to my office was preparatory to deciding whether to decide; whether to accept responsibility for shaping her own future, or go on as she had before, letting others decide for her.

Remember that bad days can be either bothersome and distracting annoyances along life's "yellow brick road," or opportunities to carve a different future. Christina's bad days, from my limited view, pointed toward opportunity. They flashed the red warning lights that indicated danger ahead, pointing to a needed detour in this young secretary's life. The yellow brick road of her dreams had developed hazardous potholes. Her bad days seemed to say, "Christina, you can't go on with your life without making some big changes."

And Christina was answering back, "I don't know if I have the courage and the strength."

Whatever she decided, Christina would be choosing her own future in the days to come.

Let's take another example, perhaps more in tune with your experience. Suppose you feel resentful toward a friend because he or she doesn't seem to be giving much to the friendship anymore. You do all the inviting while your friend does all the taking. At first this was a minor irritation; now it has become a major resentment. And that resentment has created a number of bad days. You feel angry and even hostile, but these feelings don't do much more than swirl around in your head. Instead of going away, the resentment grows.

You've got two choices: to deal with this resentment or continue to do nothing. The choice to do nothing creates the risk of continued resentment and possibly the termination of the friendship. Doing nothing is clearly a decision about the future. The other choice is to take a risk and try to work out the conflict. The first non-decision gives in to the crisis; the "try to do something" decision seizes upon the crisis as an opportunity to restore a bruised friendship. If you accept the challenge to take charge of this situation, then you advance to the next logical stage of the decision-making process.

Stage 2. Searching for Alternatives

Choosing our own future is deciding what we want and then choosing how we want to achieve it. Some call it goal-setting. It's the familiar "ends and means" idea that philosopher John Dewey talked about. Every day we set goals for ourselves and try to meet them. Some we achieve; others we don't. Some routine decision-making is a habit—a routine as simple as buying a loaf of bread. We need a loaf of bread. To get a loaf of bread, we have to go to a bakery where bread is made and sold. Which bakery? How to get there? All are routine and automatic decisions we make in order to arrive at the goal—a loaf of bread.

Routine decision-making in getting a loaf of bread can become more complex if we get to the bakery and discover that it's closed. The goal is still to get a loaf of bread because we've unexpectedly run out or guests are coming. But if it's a holiday, the means to the end may not be so easy. We may have to look at a number of alternatives—searching for an open store, borrowing from neighbors, or baking the bread at home.

To go back to Christina's example, she wanted more freedom in her life—a goal. Ah, but how to get it! The benefits carried a price tag. Still, she began to list the alternative means of attaining her goal—freedom. Some of them were:

1. Move out of parents' home and into own apartment.
2. Move to a different city.
3. Change from being a secretary to a different job.
4. Begin psychotherapy.
5. Continue present life-style.
6. Move in with boyfriend.

At this stage in decision-making, evaluation is less important than producing as many ideas as possible. Evaluation comes later.

In the second example—the hypothetical resentment you feel toward a friend—healing the friendship may be your goal. Imagine that you're tired of doing all the inviting; you want your friend to invite you sometimes.

Now comes the important and difficult task of listing ways you might reach that objective. Remember not to criticize or evaluate your list on this go-round. The following might be a few of the alternatives:

1. Don't make a fuss, and continue as you have been.
2. Stop calling your friend.
3. Get somebody to talk to your friend on your behalf.
4. Throw a big dinner party and don't invite your friend.
5. Sit down with your friend and share your feelings.

You could probably add your own suggestions to that list of ideas. Again, write down as many suggestions as you can without judging them. Sometimes, the act of writing down your ideas will help you see your objective differently. You may discover that being invited to your friend's home for dinner is not really what you want—that you just want your friend to call you once in a while. As you build your list of potential solutions, look for the not-so-obvious alternative that could be just the right choice.

Stage 3. Evaluating Alternatives

Methods for sifting and sorting through your list of ideas can be as complex or as simple as you want them to be. If the scheme is too complex, you may get bogged down in details and give up in frustration. Or, if it's too simple, you may be tempted to be haphazard about the process.

I favor a modified Wheeler and Janis approach, which lets an idea for a solution sift through four clarifying questions that will lay out the advantages and disadvantages of each alternative. Ask yourself, "If I follow this alternative . . ."

1. "What will be the tangible results for me?"
2. "What will be the tangible results for my friends and family?"
3. "What will be the impact on my self-worth?"
4. "What will others think of me?"

Let's see how this sifting and sorting technique might work in Christina's example. The first idea in her list of alternatives was "move out of parents' home and into own apartment."

I. *Tangible results for me?*
   a. I will feel lonely.
   b. It will cost more to live in my own apartment.
   c. I won't have to account to anyone in the evening.
   d. I can make own decisions—come and go as I please.

II. *Tangible results for friends and family?*
   a. More freedom to be with friends.
   b. Parents will probably miss my companionship.
   c. Less work for my mother.

III. *Impact on my self-worth?*
   a. I'll feel independent.
   b. I hope I'll feel less guilty about "not growing up."
   c. No one can take care of me, but me.

IV. *What others will think of me?*
   a. Some will be happy.
   b. Some may think I've abandoned my parents.
   c. I *hope* my parents will be supportive of me.
   d. My parents will probably miss me but may respect my new independence.

After putting each alternative through this battery of questions, the next step is to put a plus or minus sign before each answer, deciding later how important you consider any advantage or disadvantage. The idea is not to come up with a completely objective and fool-proof system of making choices, but to weigh possible alternatives to see if any rise to the top. Even though we use the best of techniques, any human decision that has a chance of being successful will also involve the risk of failure, of not working out as we intended it.

Of course, we hope to minimize risks. That's where we depend on friends and experts to be a sounding-board for ideas. If we have a medical problem, we go to a doctor. For a legal decision, we may consult an attorney. Professional advice-givers send bills for their counsel, but we can often get expert, and caring, advice from people who don't charge for it. A phone call to just the right person can often help us make a decision. Don't overlook your friends. They probably have lots of suggestions. They certainly like to give advice, and they may even try to make the decision for you in their enthusiasm to help. But resist! Whatever the decision, you're the one who will have to live with it. So let it be yours.

Let's now go back to the "negligent friend" illustration (or make up your own) and take the first alternative through each of the four evaluating questions. But this time, try your own hand at it. Remember the goal: you want your friend to invite you over sometimes. The first idea for dealing with that was to "Not make a fuss and continue as I have been." Now, under each of the following questions, list all the possible results of following that action:

I. *Tangible results for me?*
   a. _____
   b. _____
   c. _____
   d. _____

II. *Tangible results for friends and family?*

    a. _____

    b. _____

    c. _____

    d. _____

III. *Impact on my self-worth?*

    a. _____

    b. _____

    c. _____

    d. _____

IV. *What others will think of me?*

    a. _____

    b. _____

    c. _____

    d. _____

Now put a plus or minus sign before each of the above answers to see what value you place upon this alternative. Then go to the next idea on the list, and analyze it the same way, until you've completed the entire list. One alternative will probably pop out as the one best suited to your objective, leading to the next stage in this process of choosing the future of your friendship.

Stage 4. Becoming Committed

There comes a point when we have done all we can to make a good decision. We've done our homework, and the next step is leaping out into the unknown of whether a choice will be good or bad. The basic question is: "Have I done the right thing?" A yes brings satisfaction; a no can bring on feelings of guilt or depression. Whatever the choice—once we've decided to act upon it—that first moment of accountability and freedom is indeed lonely. We become painfully aware that we are responsible for the choice, and both exhilarated and terrified at our freedom for success or failure.

"Commitment does not usually come about in a flash," warn Wheeler and Janis. It's a combination of our internal readiness and motivation and our specific external actions. Commitment is sometimes so fragile that we have to reinforce our courage with symbols that prod and remind us. For instance, we can make the decision to quit smoking, but unless we take actions to reinforce that decision—like telling people about it, stocking up on chewing gum, and destroying our secret stash of cigarettes—the choice runs a high risk of failure.

Suppose Christina decided that the best choice for her was to move out of her parents' house and into her own apartment. Fearful as she was of the decision, she could tell her friends about it. Probably most would be supportive and encouraging. Undoubtedly her friends' disapproval, should she reverse her decision, would be enough to carry her through any hesitation about going ahead.

In the "negligent friend" example, what external actions might you take to help you carry through the decision that came out of stage 3?

One of the most powerful obstacles in making decisions and acting upon them is the fear of failure. It's a universal fear because no one wants to fail, especially in our success-oriented society. Failure wounds pride and self-esteem. Many people conclude that the best way not to fail is to do nothing. A lot of procrastination goes on because of the fear of failure. Either way, there's a risk. You can't fail if you haven't tried to succeed—but you can't succeed if you haven't risked failure. Furthermore, procrastination breeds guilt, resentment, and more procrastination. Many people would rather play it safe and do nothing about resolving a poor relationship with a friend or co-worker. But the resulting build-up of resentment, frustration, and tension may cause an explosion that will permanently damage the relationship. An earlier decision to risk failure is more likely to produce success and improve the basis of the friendship.

Stage 5. *Sticking to the Decision*

Stick with your decision until it no longer serves its purpose or until another decision takes its place. But beware of what Wheeler and Janis call an "impulsive reversal"; that is, following a course of action, finding it isn't working, and suddenly making a panic-stricken reversal in the opposite direction. Impulsive reversal is a desperate attempt to salvage a good decision that has soured.

For example, if Christina had moved from her parents' house into her own apartment, and her fear of loneliness came true, she might suddenly want to give up her apartment and move back with her parents, forgetting all the benefits that had come because of her new independence. That's impulsive reversal.

When a good decision doesn't seem to be working out, be on the lookout for those bad-day feelings of worry, anxiety, loneliness, and fear—especially second-punch fears. It's this add-on panic that's at the heart of impulsive reversal. For choices that have to be sustained over a long period, sticking to a decision may indeed be difficult—like dieting, quitting smoking, not drinking, or saving more of your paycheck. Wheeler and Janis recommend two common supportive techniques to help you stick with a good decision, despite the bad days that may immediately follow it.

Positive self-talk. We've all seen people walking down the street or waiting for a bus and talking to themselves. Self-talk is a way of saying to ourselves what we believe to be the benefits of following through on a choice we've made. If it's quitting smoking and we're tempted to pick up a cigarette after dinner, self-talk can help us reassert our control in a hazardous situation. It's a way of reaffirming our good intentions by keeping the issue clearly in sight. The sound of your own voice, a restatement of what you've decided, may be just enough to carry you over a lapse in your resolve. In both Christina's example and that of the negligent friend, self-talk could be a useful technique for getting through loss of nerve.

The buddy system. Anyone who has ever gone swimming at youth camp knows the buddy system. It's pairing up with a friend to look out for each other. In support groups for dieting and staying off alcohol or drugs, the buddy system helps members through temptations. In Christina's example, where the fear of loneliness could persuade her to reverse her decision, she could ask a friend to be her "buddy" over the difficult humps. Or if she went into psychotherapy, her counselor could provide this needed support.

It is possible to set up your own buddy system, say Wheeler and Janis. "But to do it you must take the lead in figuring out what would be helpful for your buddy to do and in working out an arrangement with your buddy to ensure that he or she does it." This means selecting the right person, one who will follow through on a commitment to help and be assertive in his or her support.

In a crisis, we need support, not pity.

Then work out your plan for support. Identify the difficult times when you need extra encouragement. Then arrange to meet or talk with your support friend at some time during those difficult hours.

Unless a longer space has been mutually negotiated, let these moments of "checking in" be brief and to the point. The buddy system is useful to help you through awkward spells only, and should not become a permanent crutch.

If today is a bad day for you—frustrating, resentful, threatening, or lonely—you probably made some choices that put your day on "tilt," or else you need to make some choices to get your future days going again. Think of all the times you made your own frustrating or resentful days because you were too hurried, too scared, too unsure, or too careless to make a careful decision. Remember that your biggest obstacle is deciding to decide. From then on, decision-making is setting a goal, listing alternatives, selecting one, and sticking with it.

If the choice is a good one, enjoy the success. Even if it fails, take courage in having taken a risk, learned from it, and accepted the challenge of shaping your own future.

10

Laughing at the Ridiculous

I've liked Erma Bombeck ever since she predicted thirty years ago that I would someday be a great writer. Her prophetic "Keen Teens" column with my picture and name in bold type is framed on my office wall. When writer's cramp makes my fingers stiff on bad days, I try to savor the nationally syndicated author's 1950 prediction right there on the same page as Walter Winchell's "On Broadway" column. A fledgling reporter in Dayton, Ohio, at the time, Erma wrote:

> Eager for the flow of printer's ink in their veins are Carolyn Frank and Jim Sparks. . . . Jim, author of the Pilot's "Spark Plugs" has started another "big deal" . . . interviewing celebrities by mail. Thus far, his mailbox is still awaiting replies from Mrs. Harry Truman and Herbert Hoover.[1]

Maybe that's a bit short of what I had hoped, but it's at least encouraging.

Erma Bombeck, whose business is helping Americans laugh at their bad days, portrays weekly a state of national helplessness—familiar to anyone who has ever been upset, frustrated, or angry. In one of her books she described Edward C. Phlegg, developer of Suburan Gems and builder of her house, who . . .

> made Howard Hughes look like an exhibitionist. No one had ever seen him. His phone number was a candy store that took messages. The billboards bearing his picture showed only the back of his head.
>
> "If it's an emergency," said my husband, "I suppose I could track him down."
>
> "Well, every time I push down the toaster, the garage door goes up. The hot-water heater is hooked up to the garden hose and I am sauteeing the lawn. The sliding-glass doors don't slide. The wall heats up when I turn on the porch light. The hall toilet does not accept tissue. Half of our driveway is on our neighbor's property, the grapes on the kitchen wallpaper are growing upside down, and I have a sign on our front door reading, "OUT OF ORDER! PLEASE USE HOUSE NEXT DOOR."[2]

Erma speaks for nearly everyone who has suffered bad days.

So does Andy Rooney. No crisis is too small. He specializes in noncrises that are "sure-fire day killers." From toothpaste tubes squeezed in the middle to mayonnaise tops on peanut butter jars—nothing escapes Rooney's sardonic wit; it's as current as this morning's predicament.

For people moved less by clogged septic tanks and more by the big crises of failure, death, and unrequited love, Woody Allen is the wispy guru for laughter to get through the next anxiety attack. Talented, eccentric, haunted by his own mortality, Allen entered the following "worry" item in his "secret private journal."

> Getting through the night is becoming harder and harder. Last evening, I had the uneasy feeling that some men were trying to break into my room to shampoo me.

But why? I kept imagining I saw shadowy forms, and at 3 A.M. the underwear I had draped over a chair resembled the Kaiser on roller skates. When I finally did fall asleep, I had that same hideous nightmare in which a woodchuck is trying to claim my prize at a raffle. Despair.[3]

"It is a form of whistling past the graveyard," a *Newsweek* cinema critic described Woody Allen's bizarre humor. Like Bombeck's preoccupation with running a house and raising a family, and Rooney's belief that modern gadgetry is out to get him, Allen has turned his fears and obsessions into quick gags which he jots down on matchbooks and napkins, eventually incorporating them in books and films.

All three humorists have made comic careers from their bad days and they help me through mine. Like the little boy or girl caught after dark along an eerie cemetery shortcut, they seem to know what it means to be alone and afraid of imaginary ghosts and giant Halloween pumpkins. They help us turn our bad days over to the irreverent, unpredictable, and ironic scrutiny of laughter—that inner whistling-past-the-graveyard that lifts the soul and comforts the exhausted, fearful, and frustrated.

Humor is what psychologist Harvey Mindess, an authority on the therapeutic uses of humor, calls "the frame of mind associated with a chuckle, a smile, or a laugh . . . conquering a specific threat or stress." He adds, "Those topics at which we laugh most heartily are all, in some way, sources of anxiety or discomfort, but as we laugh at them our anxiety lessens, our discomfort decreases."[4]

Let's explore how humor helps us through bad days and what we can do to cultivate a sense of the ridiculous.

How Humor Helps

Sometimes a day gets so incredibly bad that the only way to deal with it is to laugh or die. There's no in-between, no middle ground. And on one of those really bad days, even dying seems to take forever.

One of the terrors of my professional life as a seminar leader is to arrive for a presentation without my tools—handouts, visual aids, and anything else I might need. I'm compulsive about making sure that I carry my tools at my side when I travel.

Except once. I gambled and lost.

I was taking a small commuter plane from Milwaukee to Hayward in northern Wisconsin last spring to give a presentation. Since the plane I got on would be the one that would land at my final destination, I let the pilot carry my irreplaceable treasures on board with him. Departing more than two hours late, we flew through a thunder-storm that I later found out was on the edge of a tornado. Hastily we put down at a little airport about mid-state, where Marcie, another teacher, and I watched our luggage being carried off the airplane because, the pilot said, we were over weight. Since we would be working the next morning and needed our materials, we went up to the sympathetic, but resolute, ticket agent. She had two messages for us: (1) we would be flown to an airport that was two hours by car from the one where we were scheduled to land; and (2) our baggage would be driven forty miles to our motel the next morning. Marcie and I tried to laugh the best we could as we gave explicit descriptions of our bags to the agent and directions as to where they should be delivered.

All during dinner and the rest of the evening I was apprehensive. So was Marcie. Sleeping fitfully, I was aroused at four o'clock by a hard knock at the door. It was the airport driver delivering our luggage. He piled Marcie's boxes and suitcase at her door, and one lone bag at my door.

"You left two of my bags in your truck," I shouted through the misting fog broken only by the headlights shining into my motel room.

"Nope," he shouted. "That's all I got."

"What about my two bags I need in just a few hours?" I asked, feeling a lump beginning to form in the hollow of my stomach. "You promised to get them here. Don't you remember, I wrote down my name and descriptions on a piece of paper. Where's my piece of pa . . ." I realized that he didn't know what I was talking about. Slamming the door, I didn't know whether to go back to bed or cry. I tried to call the airport, but there was no answer.

Frustrated and disappointed, I rang Marcie's room. She had been awakened by the messenger's knock on her door. "He didn't bring my bags; what am I going to do?" I blubbered into the phone.

For a moment the receiver was dead in my ear, and then she laughed. Four o'clock in the morning and I'm feeling terrible, and Marcie laughed. Then we both laughed.

Marcie suggested that I call the area Extension person who had been with us at dinner the night before and who lived near the airport. I did—getting her out of bed at five. She graciously brought the bags to my motel, waited for me to change into fresh clothes, and we arrived just five minutes before my scheduled engagement. I was angry and exhausted. I had been on a round-the-clock bad day since the day before, and today hadn't even officially started! At the time, this experience was incredibly upsetting—a horrible, no good, very bad experience. And it probably would have ruined the whole day had it not been for Marcie, whose sense of humor lifted my own spirit as I waited for my errant luggage to catch up with me.

The feeling of helplessness and frustration at being

totally out of control is indescribable. Humor helps us cope with situations that can't be handled any other way. It can make an embarrassment or even a minor catastrophe bearable. Humor shows us the funniness of an event because it's something that everyone can share, like fooling with half-squeezed toothpaste tubes and mayonnaise tops that don't quite fit the peanut butter jar. We laugh at the predicaments of others because we have experienced the same frustrations and surprises. Humor brings us back to the roots of our common humanity. We laugh because we have felt the stirrings of basic emotions—feelings of inferiority, pity, sexuality, aggression, frustration, embarrassment, and guilt. Because humor turns up the hidden and the unexpected, we can take an ordinary event and appreciate its incongruities, that which seems out of place, a shade off-center from the usual and the expected.

To have a sense of humor is to be able to see the funny side of life—to take what's traditional, conventional, logical, and moral—and to turn it upside down. Humor probes below the surface meanings to search out the absurdities, the paradoxes, and the exaggerations. For getting through many of our bad days, like graveyards at dusk, humor is an inner whistling of the spirit that gives a sense of proportion to a bad day.

"When we operate out of our sense of humor," says Mindess, "we train a widened perspective on ourselves. We see ourselves and our lives from a certain distance, and that distance makes all the difference in the world."[5]

Cultivating a Sense of Humor

In learning to cultivate a sense of humor, don't expect overnight miracles. Changing behavior is difficult

enough, but changing attitudes is harder. To have a sense
of humor means that you nurture a playful attitude toward
life. The idea is not to make a joke of everything, but to be
serious without taking yourself too seriously. A sense of
humor may not solve problems that arise, but it can help us
live with them. Here are some suggestions for cultivating a
sense of the ridiculous.

Practice a playful spirit toward life. "The aim of our sense of
humor is not to reduce us to a childish state of mind,"
writes Dr. Mindess, "but to enliven our childhood with
injections of our childishness. Once we have acquired the
ability to take things seriously, we need to revive the
ability to take them playfully."

When seriousness and playfulness meet, the clouds
quickly lift from a sagging day. Here's an example of what
I mean. An avid mail freak, I've been known to intercept
the day's treasure of white and manila envelopes before it
leaves my office mailroom. Recently I tore into an innocent
envelope. It was from a local bar specializing in nude
entertainment. Inside were a half-dozen free admission
tickets and a cover letter explaining the reason I was the
lucky recipient. I had instructions to give these free passes
to out-of-town university visitors.

I had a different idea. What I chose to do instead was to
make the rounds of colleagues I knew to be active in the
women's movement. I had only one mission—to give
away the free passes from my "girlie show" benefactor—
and then to wait for their reactions. Though terribly
serious about the cause they enthusiastically defend, the
three victims of my perversity accepted it with the
playfulness I intended.

Spontaneous playfulness that supports a sense of
humor is risky, like reaching out to someone whose
seriousness does not let them laugh. But don't give up.
You've taken a risk, and you've discovered the person's

limits. For every rigid person you encounter, you'll find one who responds positively to a playful attitude toward life. Wit and good-natured kidding can be useful for working through new friendships. With humor and a playful spirit we can communicate the sacred as well as the profane.

Accept flaws and foolishness as a measure of your uniqueness. For years, Archie Bunker of TV's "All in the Family," has made Americans laugh with his naïveté, his absurd outlook on the world, his bigotry, and his "poor soul" posture in the face of events beyond his control. Millions laugh. Some laugh because Archie represents those "other people" (thank God I'm not like them). But many of us laugh because Archie Bunker is too much like us. His flaws and foolishness, satirized in exaggeration and the incongruous, resemble ours. He helps us see our own prejudices and stereotypes.

It's our flaws and foolishness that make us attractive to each other. People who spend their lives trying to be super-serious perfectionists are likely to be boring people. They live a robot existence and tend to color everything they touch gray. The flaws and foolishness that are uniquely ours can provide comic relief to a routine and otherwise moribund existence.

How many bad days come about because you haven't accepted yourself? Listen to how you talk. Do you berate yourself for small faults? Do you discount yourself when you make a mistake? Do you put yourself down when you think you have said or done something foolish? To accept life is to accept our own flaws and foolishness—plainly, that's who we are.

Look for the ridiculous and share it with someone. The seventeenth chapter of Genesis has an example of laughing at the ridiculous. When God told Abraham, who was ninety-nine, and his wife Sarah, who was ninety, that they would have a son born to them, Abraham listened, bowed reverently, and laughed.

In some situations that's about all we can do. Find the exaggeration and the incongruity and enjoy its humor. To look for the ridiculous is to search out the funniness of a thing without detracting from its seriousness. Sharing the absurdity with another can also help lighten a bad day. Sometimes, while there may be little humor in a frustrating or painful experience, it at least makes a funny story to laugh at later, with friends.

11

When Nothing Works—
The Art of Muddling Through

This is the safety-valve chapter. When you've tried all the sage advice in the previous pages, and nothing seems to work, then do what the British do—*muddle through.* Americans haven't yet learned this art. We still think that we can *fight* our way out of or *fix* our way through any problem, including the bad days. The June 24, 1980, issue of *Newsweek* symbolizes this "I-haven't-met-anything-I-can't-lick" attitude. Right there on the front cover was a picture of Sugar Ray Leonard, twenty-four years old and undefeated in twenty-seven professional fights. With gloves poised, in full color, Sugar Ray is described as retaining his "scrubbed and smiling innocence," with youthful charm and the "ability to make every swift step and crisp combination appear refreshing and invigorating." What else? That's what we expect of national heroes, when we can find them—innocence, charm, and the ability to leap tall buildings with a single bound.

Sugar Ray symbolizes America's fighting spirit when it comes to facing down problems. But that same issue of *Newsweek* also carried a lead commentary on this country's inability to "technofix" its way through the major problems of our time. Since Sugar Ray Leonard was soundly defeated in his fight-of-the-century with Panamanian Roberto Duran, and the major economic and international problems of the country seem to be getting worse rather than better, the great American "fix-it" myth is quickly fading. If champions like Sugar Ray, Mohammed Ali, and the good ol' USA can be defeated— what's left?

What's left is going ahead anyway, in spite of the impossible.

The British seem to have developed the ability to face the impossible and come out all right. During World War II, when the Nazis were blowing British planes out of the sky, and pounding British cities with their bombs, Winston Churchill and the British people took what seemed certain defeat and turned it into victory. Hitler was holding onto a frenzied illusion that he could bomb Britain into submission with night raids and an arsenal of bombs designed to kill and maim. But the British stiffened up, took the blitz in their stride, worked to defuse the unexploded bombs, and "muddled through" to victory.

What's left is to admit that, even though the impossible is at hand and defeat near, we have no choice but to "muddle through." When we can no longer slug it out or patch up what's broken, we've got to try a different strategy.

These pages are for those who have faced bad days that couldn't be fought through or fixed. Author Kirkpatrick Sale said in his *Newsweek* essay:

> Solutions, we must remember, are very much like problems; they are rooted in people, not in technology. Schemes that try to devise miracles to bypass people, negate, deny, nullify or minimize people, will not work—or at least they will not work on a planet on which it is people who are expected to live.[1]

Muddling through is a skill, maybe even an art. Muddling through is using whatever is at hand to deal with bad days, drawing on inner strength, making helpful decisions, and picking out the absurdities of the situation. But there's more, as we shall now see.

Let Yourself Be Human

On the surface the advice to let yourself be human sounds like a trite, obvious, and terribly simplistic statement. But many of the people I meet in my workshops have a difficult time accepting their painful feelings. It's as if they haven't really accepted their feelings and responses as normal and human. There's something within many of us that can't let us acknowledge that these are the feelings of everyday living.

Bad days can either bring out painful human feelings, or create them. Sometimes it's difficult to know whether we feel down because of the bad days, or whether we have bad days because we feel down. Which comes first doesn't matter. Don't punish yourself for being who you are.

Accept vulnerability and pain as inherent in living. We are not disembodied ghosts who float through the air free of impediments. We mortals depend on doors to help us get through walls, but sometimes we bump into them. Bumps can hurt. So can the bumps on our pride or self-esteem when people knock into us—a common human occurrence. If we accept the physical pain, why not the pain to our psyche?

Perfectionism is a widespread malady in our society. It pushes people to reach beyond their human limits. Different from a healthy pursuit of excellence, the pursuit of perfection pushes some people to strain compulsively and unremittingly toward impossible goals. It can contribute to bad days because they feel they haven't measured up, and have indeed failed.

Accepting yourself as a human being means that sometimes you have to get along without an answer, a solution, or an assurance. Life is imperfect, and so are we. The task is not to strive for perfection, but to be as creative as possible with the incomplete, the imperfect, and even the impossible.

Know and Accept Your Limitations

This is the next logical step in muddling through: realizing that being human carries certain non-negotiable limitations. We could avoid much pain, and deal with life's bad days, if we could only accept our limitations. But the need to be perfect—the neurotic obsession with being first, or best, or flawless—too often compels us to always be in control. People who need absolute order in their lives get upset and nervous when something goes wrong. In defense, they try to hold on tighter, making themselves more miserable and sometimes losing their grip altogether. A colleague I interviewed gave this example:

A young woman I know has been a household perfectionist since she was small. Her own parents had allotted chores to their children and demanded absolute perfection in this housework every Saturday—if there were dust motes under the bed or streaks on the mirrors, they couldn't go out to play for the rest of the day.

Recently, this woman's sister came to visit. Planning for a Monday night arrival time, she had taken apart her house to make sure every inch of it was spotless for her sister's visit. When she heard from her sister on Saturday that she was coming two days early, she flew into a panic, cancelled an invitation to celebrate her parents-in-law's 40th

131

wedding anniversary, and grew hysterical over the amount of work to be done.

Someone with a sense of humor and an attitude that to be human is to be imperfect would have muddled through, making things tidy . . . would have told her sister that her early arrival meant the house would not be perfectly in order . . . or even put her sister to work helping when she arrived. As it was, this perfectionist fell apart, ruined her in-laws' anniversary, and was miserable for most of her sister's visit because things weren't as totally spotless as she'd expected.

One of our limitations is our inability to control the opinions others have of us. The more contact we have with people, the more they will learn about us, and the more there will be to like or dislike. Image-making in political campaigns is a fascinating example of how a few try to manipulate the masses to show off a candidate in the best light. At best, the results are temporary; the candidate's personality, frankness, and record are the most powerful shapers of what people think.

Another limitation is our biology. Our bodies link us to a natural system in which plants, animals, and people live for a time, sicken, and die. The biological limitations of the natural world circumscribe our lives, determining what we will look like, our height, our intellect, and, to a great extent, our health. In our bodies are both the capacity for renewal and the necessity for decay. When cells cease to renew themselves, decaying begins, and death comes. No matter how hard we try, how much we pray or hope, some disease, accident, or old age will eventually kill us. We stand by helplessly while a friend slowly dies, or we wait out each step of a disease in our own bodies—feeling helpless and angry with our human limitations.

The limitations of our biology also dog us as we go through the life cycle from birth to death, as we observe the seasons, as we go from night to day, as we experience hunger and sleepiness. The cycle of the year and the seasons play important roles in our individual daily rhythms—the ebb and flow of our energy, enthusiasm, and creativity. I know, for instance, that if I drastically interrupt my sleep routine, the next day or two are thrown off balance. Or if I miss an exercise period at the gym, the rest of the day just doesn't feel right.

Muddling through an "impossible" situation or problem means that we listen to our body rhythms so that we try to tackle the tough issues at high strength, at the peak of our energy, rather than when we feel all washed out.

Let Some Puzzles Be Unfinished

We create many bad days for ourselves by thinking we must have a solution or a fix for everything. It's the great big American "fight it or fix it" fantasy I've already referred to. I see it in a lot of people, and I see it in myself. We think we can't go on if we can't answer a question, solve a problem, or make a bad day better.

Unresolved misunderstandings between people are a common source of unfinished puzzles in our lives. In some situations, people react and feelings flare. Marriages strain, and friendships break up. Misunderstandings and conflicts create a lot of hurt, and relationships sometimes can't be mended. The puzzle remains unfinished.

I talked recently with a Florida couple who were terribly agonized about a conflict that had developed between them and a neighbor. The cause of the difficulty seemed silly, but had severed an important friendship. Mike and Rosalie wanted to find the missing piece to the puzzle and restore the friendship. But nothing seemed to work. What to do?

At some point we had to face the issue: "What if this situation can't be fixed?" They didn't want to accept that possible reality. They believed that somewhere there was an answer, if they only searched long and hard enough. But sometimes the search ends nowhere. The conflict may never get resolved. There may never be an answer.

Nevertheless, muddling through means relaxing from trying to achieve some impossible goals so you can pursue other opportunities.

Get a Good Night's Sleep

Thomas A. Edison, according to his wife, would each evening go over in his mind the things he hoped to accomplish the next day. Then the next morning he would be fresh and ready for each task noted on his list. The inventor's well-known cat-naps caused one observer to say about Edison: "When stumped by something, he would stretch out in his Menlo workshop and, half-dozing, get an idea from his dream mind to help him around the difficulty."

Whatever the reason for our bad days, it's likely to demand our total thinking energy until we think of nothing else. If it's resentment, we roll it around in our heads until we become obsessed. If it's a criticism, we take the critic's message and "do a number on ourselves." If it's the health of a parent or child, we let our worries and fears consume us. Relying on the great American "fight it or fix it" myth, we hope that if we think about something hard enough and long enough, it will either go away or get solved.

But conscious, intensive thinking keeps the problem in that part of the brain that searches for the rational, logical solution. When that search is frustrated or confused, as some problems turn out to be, we may work even harder to solve them and become more nervous and upset. The surgeon and author Maxwell Maltz wrote:

> If you have been wrestling with a problem all day without making any apparent progress, try dismissing it from your mind, and put off making a decision until you've had a chance to "sleep on it." Remember that your creative mechanism works best when there is not too much interference from your conscious "I." In sleep, the creative mechanism has an ideal opportunity to work independently of conscious interference, if you have previously started the wheels turning.[2]

The evidence for the usefulness of "relaxing into a problem" is impressive. Many inventors, writers, engineers, and scientists tell how they went to bed with a perplexity, and rose the next day with an answer. Others arise from sleep in the middle of the night to jot down ideas and solutions to perplexing problems. In his advice to young writers, Rudolf Flesch describes the "that's it!" phenomenon:

> The conscious mind, of course, is always more orderly than the unconscious. That's why the unconscious is so much better at combining ideas in a novel way. It puts things together that we never would put together "in our right mind." As long as we pay attention to what we are doing, we just cannot make ourselves combine two ideas that, offhand, don't seem to fit together. But when the mind is busy with something else, or when we are relaxing or asleep, anything goes. Our unconscious just keeps toying with idea combinations regardless of whether they make sense or not. And then—"out of nowhere"—comes the flash of inspiration.[3]

Muddling through the bad days helps us concentrate less on worrying out a solution, and more on being ready to follow up on "surprise ideas." It's different from giving in or giving up on bad days. Muddling through means you look for the unexpected; in some instances, you even create an answer or a solution. You don't wait for bad days to get better; you reach out to them with inner strength, problem-solving, humor, and a willingness to be surprised when nothing seems to work out as you expected.

Worry About Only One Problem at a Time

'Tis easier said than done to worry about only one problem at a time. Things that really get to us usually come in bunches. When we hurt and feel upset, it's usually the aggregate of problems that weighs us down, rather than any single one. We feel like there's one big gray "blob" hanging over us. For example, Mother calls to complain that you've been neglecting her. Why don't you write or visit more often? The neighbor has complained that your cat dug up her flowers, and if you don't do something she will call the police. And the committee meeting you went to—the chairperson rambled on and nothing got done. What a day!

Each one of these is deserving of being worried over all by itself. *Don't ruin one good worry by lumping too many problems together.*

Then there's that feeling of guilt that nearly anyone can produce on demand. Guilt can add on any number of worries that would never occur at other times. The phone call from Mother reminds you of other times you didn't write or call. Or the neighbor's complaint uncovers hidden anger that you'd forgotten, or digs up buried irritation over some of her habits you'd been kind enough to ignore.

For people who do a lot of worrying, taking problems one at a time means you can spread them out, so you don't have to worry about what to do when you have nothing more to worry about!

Find a Listening Friend

A friend is someone who accepts you the way you are—someone you can accept without wanting to change that person. Friends enjoy each other in the good times, as well as in the bad. Whatever the chemistry underlying the friendship—that mysterious mixture of personality, idiosyncracy, and circumstance—there's nothing like a good friend for bad days.

"A number of times in my life I have felt myself bursting with insoluble problems," says Carl Rogers, a counselor's counselor, "or going round and round in tormented circles, or during one period, overcome by feelings of worthlessness and despair, sure I was sinking into psychosis." He continues:

> I think I have been more lucky than most in finding at these times individuals who have been able to hear me and thus to rescue me from the chaos of my feelings. I have been fortunate in finding individuals who have been able to hear my meanings a little more deeply than I have known them. These individuals have heard me without judging me, diagnosing me, appraising me, evaluating me. They have just listened and clarified and responded to me at all the levels at which I was communicating. I can testify that when you are in psychological distress and someone really hears you without passing judgment on you, without trying to take responsibility for you, without trying to mold you, it feels *damn good*.[4]

The friend that you or I choose may not quite measure up to the Rogers' ideal, but even if he or she came only modestly close, that would be some friend indeed.

How can talking through the bad days with a friend help? There are two ways. First, talking helps diffuse intense feelings of anger or fear. You feel better because you have shared your burden with another person. "How good it feels to get that off my chest," you say with a deep sigh. But there has to be more than just talking. There also has to be understanding from the listener. If just talking helped, you could talk into a tape recorder or to a tree. "Creative, active, sensitive, accurate, empathetic, non-judgmental listening," says Rogers, "is for me terribly important in a relationship. It has been extremely important especially at certain times in my life to receive it. I feel that I have grown within myself when I have provided it."

Talking with an understanding friend gives another benefit—it provides a sounding board for testing ideas. A good listener will be slow to advise, and quick to help clarify questions and tentative answers. Just being there with you as you muddle through a bad day—working over the perplexities, struggling with the feelings, trying out solutions—is the role of a listening friend.

To expect more only prolongs your misery, and abuses the friendship. Friends can help you bear the burden, but don't expect them to carry it *for* you. You can't pass your problems off on them; merely ask them to share and help you find solutions. Friends who are good listeners may lack assertiveness, the ability to say "no" or set limits in a friendship. They don't want to appear insensitive and uncaring. But too much talking about the bad days, especially if it isn't balanced with celebrating the good ones, just worries the problem and bores the listener. People who listen for a living—mental health professionals—believe that setting limits on their listening time is part of the healing process, and that total availability only prolongs dependency. People get well faster and work harder on getting through their bad days when time and money are limited. Though friends don't charge for their time or set limits on it, the same principle applies.

Pray

You don't have to be "religious" to pray. Nor do you have to do it very well. Some of the most helpful prayers I've heard have come from people who stumbled around for something to say. The stumbling and hesitancy fit the intensity of the moment; an illness, a death, a crisis that disorganizes everyone. The really important prayers, the most meaningful, are probably ninety-five percent "stumble" and five percent well-organized thoughts.

Even if you are an outright atheist or agnostic, it's never too late to pray, even if you've never done it before. Nor need you feel guilty if you are embarrassed and feel awkward. Bad days may lead to patience, hope, and faith through such effort.

In a Nazi prison awaiting death for plotting to overthrow Hitler, Dietrich Bonhoeffer wrote: "I believe God will give us all the power we need to resist in all times of distress. But he never gives it in advance, lest we should rely upon ourselves and not on him alone."[5]

To pray through the bad days is not a sign of defeat. It's a way of reaching out of our human limitations toward One who stands with us in our deepest needs.

In these pages I have argued that the bad days are as much a part of our lives as the good ones. Bad days, one at a time or in groups of two, three, or more, often catch us off guard, intruding upon our happiness, and robbing us of our joy. Because each bad day is unique, reaching out to it and living it cannot be left to chance. Some bad days we can fight or fix our way through. Others we deal with by finding the right solution or decision. Some bad days we can only laugh at. And still a smaller number strike us dumb because of their complexities—defying all reason and accepted strategies. They don't respond to good advice or the most carefully laid plans. For those bad days, our only alternative is to muddle through, hoping that God in his time will reveal their *meaning*, if not their solution.

Notes

Introduction

1. E.F. Schumacher, *A Guide for the Perplexed* (New York: Harper & Row, 1977), p. 24.
2. Jürgen Moltmann, *The Passion for Life* (Philadelphia: Fortress Press, 1978), pp. 25–26.
3. Jean-Paul Sartre, *No Exit and Three Other Plays* (New York: Vintage Books, 1946), p. 47.
4. Moltmann, *Passion for Life*, p. 23.

1 Frustration

1. Andy Rooney, "You Can Depend On . . .," *Wisconsin State Journal* (July 1, 1980), p. 3.
2. Hans Selye, *Stress Without Distress* (New York: New American Library, 1974), p. 75.
3. Martin E. Marty, "M.E.M.O.," *The Christian Century*, vol. XCVII (January 2-9, 1980), p. 31.
4. Arthur Bloch, *Murphy's Law and Other Reasons Why Things Go Wrong* (Los Angeles: Price/Stern/Sloan Publishers, 1980), p. 11.
5. Selye, *Stress Without Distress*, p. 76.
6. Wayne E. Oates, *Workaholics, Make Laziness Work For You* (Nashville: Abingdon, 1979), p. 122.
7. Eric Berne, *Games People Play: The Psychology of Human Relationships* (New York: Grove Press, 1964), pp. 73–91.

2 Resentment

1. Leo Madow, *Anger* (New York: Charles Scribner's Sons, 1972), p. 3.

2. "Secretary on the Spot," in *The Secretary* (January, 1977), p. 32.
3. Adelaide Bry, *How to Get Angry Without Feeling Guilty* (New York: New American Library, 1976), pp. 134–42.
4. Bry, *How to Get Angry*, p. 116.
5. Madow, *Anger*, p. 71.
6. Rolland S. Parker, Ph.D., *Emotional Common Sense* (New York: Harper & Row, 1973), pp. 114–21.

3   Threats

1. John Russell Taylor, *Hitch: The Life and Times of Alfred Hitchcock* (New York: Berkeley Books, 1980), p. 319.
2. Rollo May, *The Meaning of Anxiety* (New York: Simon & Schuster, 1979), p. xx.
3. Eugene Kennedy, *The Trouble Book* (New York: Simon & Schuster, 1976), p. 127.
4. Dr. Claire Weekes, *Peace from Nervous Suffering* (New York: Hawthorn Books, 1972), p. 28.
5. Andy Rooney, *Chicago Tribune* (October 5, 1980).

4   Loneliness

1. Harold Blake Walker, "Lonely Hunters," *Chicago Tribune Magazine,* (March 16, 1980), p. 12.
2. Zick Rubin, "Seeking a Cure for Loneliness," *Psychology Today,* vol. 13 (October, 1979), pp. 82–90.
3. Rubin, "Seeking a Cure for Loneliness," pp. 82–90.
4. Terri Schultz, *Bittersweet: Surviving and Growing from Loneliness* (New York: Penguin Books, 1978), p. 4.
5. Clark Moustakas, *Loneliness* (New York: Prentice-Hall, 1961), pp. 5–7.
6. Schultz, *Bittersweet,* p. 129.
7. Carolyn Slaby, "Living in Crystal," *Women: A Journal of Liberation,* vol. 5, p. 24.
8. Rubin, "Seeking a Cure for Loneliness," pp. 82–90.
9. Wayne E. Oates, *Nurturing a Silent Heart in a Noisy World* (Garden City, N.Y.: Doubleday & Co., 1979), p. 25.
10. Henri J.M. Nouwen, *Reaching Out* (New York: Doubleday & Co., 1975), p. 28.
11. Robert Cross, *Chicago Tribune Magazine* (October 5, 1980), pp. 32 ff.
12. Ann Morrow Lindbergh, *Gift From the Sea* (New York: Random House, 1975), p. 42.

5 Giving In to Bad Days

1. Paul Reps, *Zen Flesh, Zen Bones: A Collection of Zen and Pre-Zen Writings* (Garden City, N.Y.: Doubleday & Co., n.d.), p. 71.
2. Ernest Gordon, *Through the Valley of the Kwai* (New York: Harper, 1962). A rare account of courage and compassion.

6 Grabbing Convenient Excuses

1. Robert MacKenzie, *"Review"*: Andy Rooney of "60 Minutes," in *TV Guide*, vol. 28, (October 4, 1980), p. 1.
2. Wayne Dwyer, *Your Erroneous Zones* (New York: Avon Books, 1977), p. 152.
3. Leslie D. Weatherhead, *Why Do Men Suffer?* (Nashville: Abingdon Press, 1936), pp. 106–22.

7 Leaning on Crutches

1. Donald B. Ardell, *High Level Wellness: An Alternative to Doctors, Drugs and Disease* (Emmaus, Penn.: Rodale Press, 1977), p. 53.
2. Everett L. Shostrom, *Man, the Manipulator* (New York: Bantam Books, 1968), pp. xi–xii.
3. Betty Eppes, "A Frozen Moment in Time—Talking with J.D. Salinger," *Baton Rouge Sunday Advocate Magazine* (June 29, 1980).
4. Dwyer, *Your Erroneous Zones*, p. 72.
5. Merle Shain, *When Lovers Are Friends* (Philadelphia: J.B. Lippincott Co., 1978), p. 15.

8 What Bad Days Teach Us

1. Robert E. Gard, *An Innocence of Prairie* (Madison: R. Bruce Allison, 1978), p. 31.
2. Herman Hesse, *Siddhartha* (New York: New Directions Publishing Co., 1951), p. 116.

9 Choosing Our Own Future

1. Daniel D. Wheeler and Irving L. Janis, *A Practical Guide for Making Decisions* (New York: The Macmillan Co., 1980), p. 3.

10   *Laughing at the Ricidulous*

1. Erma Bombeck, *Journal Herald* (September 23, 1950).
2. Erma Bombeck, *The Grass Is Always Greener over the Septic Tank* (Greenwich: Fawcett Publications, 1976), pp. 49–50.
3. Woody Allen, *Without Feathers* (New York: Warner Books, 1975), p. 7.
4. Harvey Mindess, *Laughter and Liberation* (Los Angeles: Nash, 1971). p. 144.
5. Mindess, *Laughter and Liberation p. 216.*

11   *When Nothings Works—*
The Art of Muddling Through

1. Kirkpatrick Sale, "The 'Miracle' of Technofix," *Newsweek* (June 23, 1980), p. 12.
2. Maxwell Maltz, *Psycho-Cybernetics* (New York: Simon & Schuster, 1969), p. 91.
3. Rudolf Flesch, *The Art of Readable Writing* (New York: The Macmillan Co., 1962), p. 59.
4. Carl R. Rogers, *Freedom to Learn* (Columbus, Ohio: Charles E. Merrill Publishing Co., 1969), p. 225.
5. Dietrich Bonhoeffer, *Letters and Papers from Prison* (London: SCM Press, 1956), p. 21.